THE NAPLES PHILHARMONIC LEAGUE
AND
THE FRIENDS OF ART

Present

The Art of Cooking ™

From Michele Marker
12/2002

Underwritten, in part, by Waterside Shops at Pelican Bay

Published by
Gulfshore Life
Naples, Florida

Produced by
Morris Press Cookbooks
Kearney, Nebraska
Printed in Korea

First Printing   10,000 copies   November 2002   ISBN: 0-9705158-3-9

Dear Creative Cooks,

COOKING CAN BE ONE OF the most creative of all the arts – and certainly the most delicious. The recipes in *The Art of Cooking* represent a wide variety of culinary delights contributed by many of our patrons and friends.

Several years ago, members of the Philharmonic League produced our first cookbook, which was a tremendous success. Now the League and the Friends of Art have teamed up to create a second one. The response to this new cookbook has been overwhelming – with more than 800 recipes submitted.

You will probably recognize the cover art. It is Don Eddy's painting *Dreamreader's Harvest*, from our exhibition *Photorealism: The Liff Collection*, which was on display at the Naples Museum of Art.

It is our longstanding mission at the Philharmonic Center to bring to our community the very best of all the arts. Therefore it makes sense to present a book on the art of cooking. I love cooking and love to collect recipe books. This is one cookbook you'll want to save – and share – for years.

Thanks to everyone who participated.

Happy cooking – and eating!

Myra Janco Daniels

Myra Janco Daniels
Chairman, President and CEO
Philharmonic Center for the Arts

A Delicious Duet

THE NAPLES PHILHARMONIC LEAGUE, ORIGINATED BY MYRA JANCO DANIELS IN 1986, began as a volunteer group of 49 orchestra subscribers, which supported the then-fledgling Naples Philharmonic Orchestra.

This ambitious group has grown to almost 700 members, who have raised more than $3 million! These funds support the orchestra and underwrite many of its youth music education programs – including the Magic Carpet Series for very young children, trips to the Phil for elementary school children and the Major/Minor Concerts featuring the Philharmonic Youth Orchestra.

Volunteering for the Phil is a very gratifying experience – especially when we see the growth of the orchestra and the joy in the faces of children experiencing music.

Our signature fund-raising event is the annual Festival of Trees, held every November. Other events include volunteering for the Dream Home and hosting the Phil Open golf outings.

This is our second cookbook but the first we have produced as a joint effort with our friends, the Friends of Art. We hope you enjoy our recipes and that *The Art of Cooking* will become one of your favorites. Bon appetit!

Grace Seitz, President, Naples Philharmonic League

THE FRIENDS OF ART WAS STARTED IN 1990 TO WORK WITH THE PHILHARMONIC Galleries, and it now also supports and complements the Naples Museum of Art. Our membership has grown from about 300 to more than 1,500.

The diversity and success of events developed by the Friends of Art has been accomplished through a spirit of mutual cooperation among the membership.

Virginia Small, president of the Friends from 1994-2002, was responsible for guiding the group through a number of important projects supporting the visual arts. Prominent lecturers from the art world, including Tom Hoving, Rosamond Bernier, Francoise Gilot and J. Carter Brown participated in lecture programs sponsored by the Friends.

Other Friends of Art events have included the popular annual Artists' Studio Tour, Living With Art, and the Chinese New Year Celebration, which raised more than $200,000 for the Museum Endowment and its education programs.

Myra Janco Daniels has been a tremendous source of inspiration and support for the Friends and we welcome her special vision in the future.

Please join us in celebrating the volunteer spirit – and enjoying some terrific recipes – in this book brought to you by the Friends of Art and the Naples Philharmonic League.

Leslie L. Branda, President, Friends of Art

Flair & Flavor

Cover artist Don Eddy brings a new meaning to the art of cooking.

Pasta with Squid & Pancetta

1/3 cup olive oil

1 (1/4-inch thick) slice pancetta, diced

1 large garlic clove, crushed

1/2 cup white wine

1 red bell pepper, peeled and diced

1/3 pound cleaned squid (bodies only) sliced in 1/8-inch ovals

1/4 cup toasted bread crumbs

1/2 pound dried shell pasta

Heat the olive oil over medium heat. Sauté pancetta until it begins to brown. Add garlic and sauté until both pancetta and garlic are golden brown. Raise heat and add both the wine and diced red bell pepper. Cook until the wine has evaporated. Add the squid and cook for 1 minute until the squid is translucent. Off heat. Cook pasta to al dente and reserve 1/4 cup liquid. Gently reheat sauce. Drain pasta. Add the pasta and 1/4 cup cooking liquid to sauce. Raise heat. Toss for 1 minute. Add the toasted bread crumbs. Toss and serve. Serves 2 as a main course and 4 as a first course.

Don Eddy, artist of Dreamreader's Harvest, *1988-89*

The Art of Cooking

Contents

ON THE COVER: Don Eddy is an internationally renowned photorealist painter. His *Dreamreader's Harvest*, 1988-89, acrylic on canvas, 50x50" appeared at the Naples Museum of Art in 2002 as part of the exhibition *Photorealism: The Liff Collection.*

The Art of Cooking

A Recipe for the Arts

THE PHILHARMONIC CENTER FOR THE ARTS IS A UNIQUE mix of some very special ingredients – generosity, vision, dedication and a deep-seated love of the arts. The Center is the result of a shared dream: to build a world-class performing arts complex in Southwest Florida. The dream became a reality in November of 1989 when the Center first opened its doors. Every year since then, both the attendance and the number of events have gone up.

The Phil is unusual among arts centers in its mission of presenting international-caliber performing and visual arts in a single complex, under a single management. Many of the leading entertainers in the world have appeared at the Phil over the years, among them Itzhak Perlman, Rudolf Nureyev, Frederica von Stade, Bill Cosby and Kiri Te Kanawa. Many of the world's leading visual artists have also appeared, along with their work, including Robert Rauschenberg, Dale Chihuly and Yaacov Agam.

In November 2000, the Philharmonic Center campus expanded with the addition of the Naples Museum of Art, Southwest Florida's first full-scale art museum.

The growth of The Phil is a mirror of the community that created it – a generous community that appreciates and nourishes the arts.

The Philharmonic Center was conceived as a permanent home for the Naples Philharmonic Orchestra (above). Dale Chihuly's stunning Red Chandelier (right) greets visitors to the Naples Museum of Art as they enter the Figge Conservatory.

The Art of Cooking

Naples Philharmonic Orchestra

THE 2002-03 SEASON MARKED THE 20TH ANNIVERSARY of the Naples Philharmonic Orchestra – the resident orchestra of the Philharmonic Center for the Arts. Begun with a handful of local musicians on Marco Island, the orchestra has grown into a nationally recognized ensemble. In recent years it has performed with such legendary singers as Luciano Pavarotti, Andrea Bocelli and Frederica von Stade and released several acclaimed CDs.

In the summer of 2002, the orchestra was featured in a nationally broadcast PBS concert, *A Century of Broadway,* with Erich Kunzel conducting.

Some highlights of the orchestra's first two decades: the formation of the Philharmonic Center Chorale in 1991; the naming of Christopher Seaman as music director and Erich Kunzel as principal pops conductor in 1993; a Grammy Award nomination in 1994 for a CD with the Manhattan Transfer; a 1997 CD released internationally on the Telarc label featuring the orchestra and renowned classical guitarist David Russell; the establishment of the Philharmonic Youth Chorale in 1998; the naming of Clotilde Otranto as resident conductor in 1999; and the establishment of the Philharmonic Youth Orchestra in 2001.

The orchestra looks toward the future with many exciting plans, as the adventure of growth continues.

The Art of Cooking

The Naples Philharmonic Orchestra appeared in the nationally televised PBS broadcast *A Century of Broadway,* which debuted in the summer of 2002, featuring pops conductor Erich Kunzel and legendary mezzo-soprano Frederica von Stade (left). Musicians from the orchestra's string, brass and woodwind sections (above and right) perform in concert at the Phil. In 2001, the Philharmonic Youth Orchestra (below) debuted, led by Resident Conductor Clotilde Otranto.

The Art of Cooking

Naples Museum of Art

A NEW ERA IN THE VISUAL ARTS BEGAN IN NOVEMBER of 2000 with the opening of the Naples Museum of Art. The region's only full-scale art museum, the Museum is a three-story, 15-gallery visual arts center dedicated to showing important painting, sculpture and drawing in a variety of styles. Artists featured in exhibitions at the Museum have included Dale Chihuly, Alice Neel, Helen Frankenthaler, Jasper Johns, Kenneth Noland, Paul Signac and many others.

In its first two seasons, the Museum garnered national and international attention – including feature stories in The New York Times, ARTnews and The Wall Street Journal.

The mission of the Museum is to enlighten, educate and enrich the community of Southwest Florida – to inspire creativity and awaken curiosity while providing educational programs and lectures along with exhibitions.

"Our objective is to be a visual arts center for people of all ages and backgrounds," said Museum founder Myra Janco Daniels. "Our most valuable assests are the support and input of our patrons."

The Naples Museum of Art brought a new experience in the visual arts to Southwest Florida. Museum visitors pass through Albert Paley's mammoth entry gates (left) en route to the Museum's 15 galleries (above), on three floors of display space. At right, a drummer from the Han dynasty is one of the many rare art objects on display in the Museum's *Gow Collection of Ancient Chinese Art*. The Pistner House (below and bottom right), one of the Museum's most popular attractions, is part of the *Masters of Miniature* exhibition.

Dale Chihuly's remarkable, other-worldly glass art (left) has captivated audiences of all ages.

A Family Affair

THE PHILHARMONIC CENTER FOR THE ARTS STRONGLY believes that the arts should be a family affair. During the 2001-02 season, 55,700 children participated in events at the Center and at the Naples Museum of Art — an increase of 13,000 over the previous year. The Phil is committed to expanding its family programming each season.

As Philharmonic Center founder Myra Janco Daniels said, "Our future is in the small hands of the children of this community."

The Phil reaches out to children in many ways — through music and art programs, partnerships with schools, special concert and theater events and more. These activities are designed to both entertain and educate, to instill in children an understanding that the arts can and should be a journey of discovery — as well as lots of fun.

The Philharmonic Youth Chorale was founded in 1998 and performs in concert with the Naples Philharmonic Orchestra.

Chorale Director James Cochran leads the Philharmonic Center Chorale. The 110-voice, all-volunteer Chorale was founded in 1991. Chorale members range from students to senior citizens.

A Philharmonic Center tradition is the Magic Carpet concert series, which allows young children to interact with Philharmonic Orchestra members — and their instruments.

13

We are
pleased to present

The
Philharmonic
Center for the Arts

BEST
PERFORMING
RECIPES

Hors d'oeuvres

Almond Stuffed Dates with Bacon
Amy's Pie
Antipasto Salad
Artichoke & Crabmeat Appetizer
Artichoke Hummus
Asparagus Spears
Bacon Bows
Baked Brie
Caviar Romanoff Pie
Cebiche de Shrimp
Cheese Biscuits
Cheese Straws
Chicken Spread
Chutney Pie
Clam Dip
Cocktail Meatballs
Cocktail Pizzas
Corned Beef Delight
Crab & Roasted Red Pepper Dip
Crabmeat Quiche
Curried Chicken Balls
Curry-Chutney Cream Cheese Dip
Eggplant Pizza
Flaming Cheese Bites
Gala Pecan Spread
Goat Cheese & Tomato Croustades
Grilled Quesadillas
Herbed Cheese Spread
Hot Claus Clam Spread
Hot Crabmeat Dip
Hot Onion Soufflé
Hot Spinach Dip
Hot Stuffed Mushrooms
Irresistible Salmon Mousse
Joanne's Cheese Balls
Liver Paté
Lou's Shrimp Dip
Mama's Crab Mornay
Mexican Layered Dip
Mushrooms Trifolati
Olive Crostini
Paté En Gelér
Pesto Dip

Reuben Dip
Sausage Stars
Shrimp Dip
Spiced Nuts
Spinach Balls
Spinach Cheese Mini Muffins
Spinach Crostini
Tomato, Onion & Anchovy Tart
Tomato Tart
Tortilla Roll-ups
Zucchini Appetizer

Drinks

Bourbon Slush
Brandy Slush
Low-cal Fruit Shake
Mango Daiquiri
Pineapple Mint Frappé
Wassail
White Sangria

Almond Stuffed Dates with Bacon

1 pound pitted dates
1 (4 ounce) package blanched
   whole almonds

13/4 pounds thinly sliced lean
   bacon

Stuff each date with an almond. Cut bacon strips into thirds and wrap a piece around each date. Secure with a round wooden toothpick. Put dates on a foil-lined baking sheet and bake in a preheated 400° oven until the bacon is crisp, about 12-15 minutes. Drain on a rack or paper towels. Serve warm or room temperature. Serves 12.

Karen Jones

Amy's Pie

5 ounces cream cheese
1/2 cup sour cream
4 teaspoons green chilies,
   chopped

1 tablespoon jalapeños, chopped
1/2 cup green onions, chopped
1 package of 10 flour tortillas
Salsa for dipping

Mix all ingredients together except salsa and spread onto 5 tortillas to make 5 thin layers. Stack and cut into pie-shaped wedges. Serve with salsa. Serves 10.

Jessica Bell

Prepared dates can be frozen in advance and baked unthawed in a preheated 400° oven until bacon is crisp.

Antipasto Salad

1/2 pound fresh mushrooms, sliced

1/2 small box cherry tomatoes, sliced

2 jars (26 ounces) sweet fried peppers

1 jar (7 ounces) roasted peppers, drained

1 small can black olives, pitted and drained

1 can artichoke hearts, chopped and drained

1 jar (9 ounces) marinated eggplant, drained

1/2 pound Swiss cheese, cut in chunks

1/2 pound Genoa salami, sliced thin, cut in strips

3 cloves garlic, minced

6 tablespoons olive oil

3 tablespoons wine vinegar

Pepper

Oregano

Toss all the ingredients together, using lots of pepper and oregano in a large bowl—should be several hours prior to serving or a day in advance. Will keep well in the refrigerator. If desired, serve with Italian breadsticks. Serves 10-12.

Sona Current

Artichoke & Crabmeat Appetizer

1 (10³/4) can of cream of mushroom soup

8 ounces softened cream cheese

1 package Knox unflavored gelatin

6 tablespoons white wine

1 cup finely chopped green onions

1 cup finely chopped celery

1 can artichokes, chopped

1 cup mayonnaise

1 pound white fresh crabmeat

2 teaspoons salt

2 teaspoons Tabasco sauce

2 tablespoons lemon juice

2 tablespoons Worcestershire sauce

Must be made the day before serving.

On top of double boiler, place soup and cream cheese. Warm and blend mixture with wire whisk. Add gelatin, which has been dissolved in white wine. Mix well and remove from heat. Add remaining ingredients and pour into well-greased 8-inch ring mold or small bundt mold. Refrigerate overnight. Unmold and garnish with stuffed green olives. Serve with crackers or toast rounds. Serves 12.

Bobi Saper

Artichoke Hummus

2 cups garbanzo beans,
  canned
1 can artichoke hearts, drained
6 cloves garlic
Juice of 2 lemons

Paprika, to taste
Cumin, to taste
Salt, to taste
White pepper, to taste
Olive oil

In a food processor mix all the above ingredients but the olive oil. Turn on and drizzle in olive oil to consistency desired. Serves 12.

Joann Duncan

Asparagus Spears

1 loaf bread
2-3 cans asparagus spears
1 package Knorr's Hollandaise
  sauce

Melted butter
Parmesan cheese

Cut crust off bread; flatten with rolling pin. Drain asparagus spears. Mix Hollandaise sauce according to directions. Brush sauce on bread. Put 1 or 2 spears on bread. Roll up in a triangle. Brush with melted butter and sprinkle with cheese. Broil until golden brown, approximately 5 minutes. Serve hot. Serves 10-15.

Laurie/Kim Biagetti

Bacon Bows

1 pound sliced bacon   36 or more Waverly crackers

Cut bacon slices into thirds. Preheat oven to 200-225°. Wrap each third of a slice tightly around a cracker. Place wrapped crackers on a rack placed on a cookie sheet or baking pan. Bake for 2 hours until slightly browned. Cool before serving. Serves 12-24.

Grace Seitz

Baked Brie

1 large wedge of brie   4 slices of cooked bacon,
1 jar Major Grey's Chutney   crumbled
2-3 chopped green onions,
   including green part

Pour chutney over wedge. Bake 5-10 minutes at 325°. Sprinkle with onion and bacon. Serve with water crackers or French bread sliced fairly thin. Serves 6-8.

Fran Gilbert

Caviar Romanoff Pie

6 hard-boiled eggs, chopped
3 tablespoons mayonnaise
1 1/2 cups onion, minced
8 ounces softened cream cheese
2/3 cup sour cream
4 ounces lump fish caviar
Parsley sprigs, to garnish
Lemon, to garnish

Combine eggs with mayonnaise. Spread over bottom of well-greased 8-inch springform pan. Sprinkle with minced onion. Blend cream cheese with sour cream. Spread over onion with spatula. Chill 3 hours or more before serving. Top with caviar spread to pan edges. Run knife around pan sides, loosen and lift. Serves 10-12.

Edna Korengold

Cebiche de Shrimp

Serve in small bowls with popcorn on the side and eat with French bread and beer. You can also substitute the shrimp with crab-meat or other seafood. A popular appetizer from Ecuador.

1 1/2 pounds frozen cooked shrimp, peeled, deveined and tail-off
1/2 pound red onions, sliced thin
1 (14 1/2 ounce) can stewed tomatoes, blend to make juice
1/2 cup ketchup
Juice of 10 lemons
Juice of 1 orange
1/2 cup olive oil
1 teaspoon mustard
1 teaspoon salt (or salt to taste)

Thaw shrimp in cold water and place in large glass bowl. Cut red onions in thin slices and boil in water for 1 minute. Drain in cold water. Place onions in another bowl and cover with lemon juice. When onion has changed color, add orange juice and stewed tomato juice. Mix well and pour over shrimp. Immediately add olive oil, ketchup, mustard and salt according to taste. Mix well and refrigerate for at least 2 hours. Serves 6.

Pablo Veintimilla

The Art of Cooking • Hors d'oeuvres & Drinks

Cheese Biscuits

1 1/2 cups flour
1/2 teaspoon salt
1/4 pound butter or margarine
1/2 pound cheddar cheese,
  grated

Dash cayenne pepper, optional
Pecan halves

Sift flour and salt together. Add softened butter, grated cheese and optional cayenne pepper. Mix well with hands to form a firm paste. Form into logs about 1 1/2 inches in diameter. Wrap in waxed paper and refrigerate overnight or until well chilled. Cut into 1/8-inch slices; place on ungreased cookie sheet. Top each with a pecan half or substitute. Bake 10-12 minutes in preheated 375° oven. Can be frozen, raw or cooked. Makes about 10 ~~dozen~~ biscuits.

Anne Ray

Cheese Straws

1/2 pound cheddar cheese,
  grated and softened to
  room temperature

4 tablespoons butter
1 cup flour, sifted
1 tablespoon baking powder

Cream cheese and butter; add flour gradually. Knead and roll out thin, cut into strips. Sprinkle with paprika. Bake 10 minutes at 400°. Sprinkle with salt. Can put everything in the processor instead of the hand method.

Ruth McNeal

Chicken Spread

This can be served with crackers as a spread or can be used as a spread between thin bread for tea sandwiches. Decorate with olives or grape tomatoes, parsley, or a twist of lemon.

3 pounds boneless chicken breasts, cooked in salt water
1 (8 ounce) package Philadelphia cream cheese
2 tablespoons Hellmann's mayonnaise
3/4 cups pecans or walnuts, chopped
1 tablespoon onion, grated
2 tablespoons sweet pickle juice
1 cup celery, chopped
1/8 teaspoon curry powder
Salt and pepper to taste

Cook chicken in salted water to cover until tender. Remove from broth, reserving broth; then cool. Bone chicken and grind or chop finely. Combine cream cheese and mayonnaise, beating well. Add pecans, onion, pickle juice, celery, curry powder, salt and pepper. Mix chicken together with cream cheese mixture and add broth to make proper consistency. Serves 24-36.

Frances Luessenhop

Chutney Pie

8 ounces cream cheese, softened
10 ounces grated sharp cheddar cheese
1 jar Major Gray's chutney
3 tablespoons sherry or bourbon
1 teaspoon curry powder
1/2 cup sliced almonds, toasted

Mix cheeses together thoroughly. Add sherry or bourbon and curry; mix well. Place in ovenproof serving dish. Let sit several hours. Top with toasted almonds. Bake for 15 minutes in 400° oven. Serve with melba rounds or low salt crackers. Makes about 3 cups.

Connie LaNier

Clam Dip

1 can minced clams
1 tablespoon clam juice
1 (3 ounce) package cream cheese, softened
2 tablespoons mayonnaise
1 teaspoon Worcestershire

Dash of Tabasco
2 teaspoons chopped scallion or onion
2 tablespoons chopped fresh parsley

Must do 1 day ahead. Doubles well.

Drain clams, reserving 1 tablespoon juice to mix with cream cheese. Mix all ingredients in order. Refrigerate 24 hours. Serve with potato chips. Serves 4.

Joyce Vitelli

Cocktail Meatballs

1 pound pork sausage
1 1/2 tablespoons chopped green onion, tops too
1/3 cup chopped pecans
1 tablespoon sherry or wine
1 egg, beaten

1/2 cup dried bread crumbs

Sauce:
1 cup orange marmalade
1/3 cup barbecue sauce

Combine first 6 ingredients. Form 1-inch balls. Bake in pan at 400° for 20 minutes. Drain. Heat the last 2 ingredients in a sauce pan. Add meatballs and bring to a simmer. Serve with toothpicks. Makes 3 dozen.

Weezie Windsor

Cocktail Pizzas

1 cup shredded mozzarella
  cheese
1 cup chopped ripe olives
3/4 cup chopped dried beef, in
  package, not jar

1 cup light mayonnaise
1 package cocktail rye bread

Mix cheese, olives, beef and mayonnaise together. Spread on rye bread. Lay on cookie sheet and bake at 350° for 15 minutes or until bubbly. Serve on a platter. Can be made ahead of time and kept in refrigerator for 1 week. Serves 24.

Jini Horan

Corned Beef Delight

Freeze leftovers on cookie sheet and then place in freezer bag. Keeps 3 to 4 months. Remove amount as needed.

1 1/2 large loaf sandwich bread
1 can corned beef
1/2 pound shredded cheddar
  cheese

1 tablespoon yellow mustard
2 tablespoons mayonnaise
Wooden toothpicks cut in half

Trim crust from bread and roll each slice thin, cut diagonally. Mix all other ingredients. Place about 1 tablespoon of mixture on bread roll and place 1/2 toothpick to hold together. Place on cookie sheet in 325° oven and bake until brown (about 6 minutes).

Lee Gates

Crab & Roasted Red Pepper Dip

1 (8 ounce) can of lump or claw crab (fresh crab is best)
1 (12 ounce) jar roasted red peppers, packed in oil, drained
Oregano (fresh or dried), to taste
Freshly cracked black pepper, to taste
1 teaspoon minced garlic, optional
Corn or tortilla chips

Chop crabmeat into bite-size pieces. Chop roasted red peppers into bite-size pieces. Mix crabmeat and roasted red peppers until thoroughly combined. Add pepper, oregano, and garlic to taste. Serve with chips. Serves 6-8.

Leslie Branda

Crabmeat Quiche

1/2 cup mayonnaise
1/2 cup milk
2 tablespoons flour
2 eggs
8 ounces fresh crabmeat
8 ounces grated Swiss cheese
8 ounces grated cheddar cheese
1/2 cup chopped onions
9-inch pie shell
1/2 teaspoon paprika

Mix mayonnaise, milk, flour and eggs until fluffy. Fold in cheese, onions and crabmeat. Spread into pie shell. Sprinkle paprika on top. Bake for 45 minutes at 350°. Serves 6-8.

Katherine Wielgus

Curried Chicken Balls

1 (8 ounce) package cream
  cheese, softened
4 tablespoons mayonnaise
2 cups chopped cooked chicken
11/4 cups almonds, finely
  chopped

3 tablespoons chopped chutney
1 teaspoon salt
2 teaspoons curry powder
1 cup grated coconut

Blend cheese and mayonnaise. Sauté almonds in 1 tablespoon butter until lightly browned, or you can brown in the oven at 350° for 10 minutes. Add almonds, chicken, chutney, salt and curry powder to cream cheese mixture. Shape into walnut-sized balls. Roll each ball in coconut. Chill until ready to serve. (Can be frozen.) Makes about 5 dozen.

Isabelle Staffeldt

Curry-Chutney Cream Cheese Dip

This is one of my favorite recipes and one always requested. It can be mixed a day ahead and stored in a covered container in the refrigerator. However, the chutney and almonds should go on just before serving.

1 large package cream cheese,
  softened
2-3 sprigs green onion
2 teaspoons Worcestershire
  sauce

1 tablespoon curry powder*
Milk
Jar of chutney
1 package slivered almonds

Blend the first 4 ingredients to proper consistency with milk as needed. Heap on serving dish. It should mound. Top with chutney and then sprinkle on the almonds. It should come out looking like a big ice cream sundae. Serve with Wheat Thins, Triskets or crackers. *If you're a curry lover add more to taste.

Gail Webster-Patterson

Eggplant Pizza

1 medium eggplant, peeled
   and cut in 3/8-inch slices
Oregano, to sprinkle
Garlic powder, to sprinkle
1 cup Italian flavored bread
   crumbs
Parmesan cheese
Tomato sauce
1/4 cup olive oil

Cut eggplant into slices and sprinkle oregano, garlic powder, bread crumbs and parmesan cheese on each piece. Place 1 tablespoon tomato sauce on top of each piece. Sprinkle more cheese and oregano on top. Sprinkle a little olive oil over all pieces. Bake at 375° for about 30 minutes or until eggplant is tender.

Helen Lavelle

Flaming Cheese Bites

11/2 pounds Kaseri cheese
11/2 cups flour
2 eggs, well beaten
1/2 cup butter
1/2 cup olive oil
1/3 cup brandy

Cut cheese in 1/2-inch cubes. Dip in flour; then egg. Flour again; egg again. End with final dip in flour. Heat butter and oil over moderate heat in frying pan. Fry until browned. Heat brandy in small pan and pour over cubes that have been put on metal plate. Flame brandy. Makes 24 bites. Serves 8.

Char Macaluso

Gala Pecan Spread

1 (8 ounce) package lowfat
cream cheese, softened
2 tablespoons milk
1/4 cup finely chopped green
pepper
1 (21/2 ounce) jar sliced dried
beef, cut up
2 tablespoons dehydrated
onion flakes

1/4 teaspoon pepper
1/2 teaspoon garlic salt
1/2 cup fat-free sour cream
1/2 cup coarsely chopped
pecans
2 tablespoons butter
1/3 teaspoon salt (use with
pecans)

Combine cheese and milk. Stir in green pepper, dried beef, onion flakes and seasonings. Fold in sour cream. Spoon mixture into an 8-inch pie plate or baking dish. Heat and crisp pecans in butter and salt. Sprinkle pecans over cheese mixture. Bake in 350° oven for 20 minutes. Serve hot with crackers. Mixture can be prepared ahead of time. Serves 8.

Judith Betsworth

Goat Cheese & Tomato Croustades

1/2 cup fresh basil leaves, packed

7 ounces mild soft goat cheese, softened

3/4 stick (6 tablespoons) unsalted butter, softened

1/2 cup sour cream

2 large eggs

18 grape tomatoes, cut in half

1 teaspoon salt

1/4 teaspoon ground black pepper

1 package Croustades

Croustades, or crispy shells, can be found in specialty stores, 24 to a package.

Chop basil. In a bowl, whisk basil and remaining ingredients. Add salt and pepper. Pour mixture into shells, filling 3/4 full. Place 1/2 grape tomato on each shell. Place on baking sheet. Bake at 350° for 15-20 minutes. Makes 24 shells.

Caroline Hinmon

Grilled Quesadillas

1 medium onion, sliced
2 tablespoons butter
8 (6-inch) flour tortillas
Olive oil
1 pound Monterey Jack cheese,
   grated

Optional additions:
Avocado slices
Sun-dried tomatoes
Sliced green chilies
Cooked shrimp, crab, lobster,
   or chicken
Sliced black olives

Sauté onion in butter and set aside. Brush one side of each tortilla with oil. Place 1/2 of the cheese on non-oiled side of 4 tortillas. Add 1/4 of the onion on top of the cheese. (May also use cheddar, brie, blue or Parmesan cheese instead of Monterey Jack. May use a combination if desired.) Add any of the optional additions. Cover with remaining tortillas. Heat charcoal or gas grill. Grill 2-3 minutes per side or until tortillas are golden brown and cheese is melted. Serves 16.

Weezie Windsor

Herbed Cheese Spread

This tastes just like boursin cheese at a fraction of the price. Food processor works best when blending ingredients.

1 (8 ounce) package cream
   cheese, softened
1 tablespoon dry vermouth
1 clove minced garlic
1/2 teaspoon dry mustard

2 teaspoons dill weed, dried
2 teaspoons parsley, dried
1 teaspoon basil, dried
1 teaspoon oregano, dried
Salt to taste

Blend all ingredients. Chill until ready to serve with crackers. Serves 8-12.

Lynn Cole

Hot Claus Clam Spread

I can minced clams with juice
I tablespoon lemon juice
1/4 pound margarine (1 stick)
I medium chopped onion
I clove crushed garlic
1/2 chopped green pepper

I teaspoon parsley
I teaspoon oregano
1/2 cup bread crumbs
1/2 cup Parmesan cheese
Paprika

Simmer clams and lemon juice for 5 minutes. Add margarine, onion, garlic, pepper, parsley and oregano. Simmer until onions and peppers are soft (5-10 minutes). Add bread crumbs. Put into a buttered pie plate. Top with Parmesan cheese and paprika. Bake 20 minutes in 350° oven. Serve hot with assorted crackers. Serves 6-8.

Lillian Kuchalla

This recipe can be made ahead of time and frozen. Adding more bread crumbs makes great stuffing for shrimp.

Hot Crabmeat Dip

I (8 ounce) package cream cheese, room temperature
I (6 ounce) can crabmeat, drained
2 tablespoons chopped green pepper
2 tablespoons chopped onion
I tablespoon cream or milk

I teaspoon prepared horseradish
1/2 teaspoon salt
I tablespoon lemon juice
1/4 teaspoon pepper
Few drops Tabasco
1/3 cup sliced almonds or chopped pecans

Mix all ingredients except nuts and place in shallow quiche or soufflé dish. Sprinkle with nuts. Bake at 375° for 15 minutes. Serve with crackers. Serves 10-12.

Theresa Hastings

Hot Onion Soufflé

12 to 16 ounces frozen chopped onions

24 ounces softened cream cheese

2 cups grated Parmesan cheese

1/2 cup Hellmann's mayonnaise

Corn chips or assorted crackers

Thaw onions. Roll them into paper towels to remove moisture. Preheat the oven to 425°. Stir together onions, cream cheese, Parmesan and mayonnaise until well combined. Transfer to a shallow 2-quart soufflé dish. Bake about 15 minutes or until golden brown. Serve with corn chips or assorted crackers. Makes about 6 cups.

Mrs. Henry Albrecht

Hot Spinach Dip

1 (8 ounce) package cream cheese, softened

1/2 cup mayonnaise

1 package (10 ounces) frozen, chopped spinach, thawed and well drained

2 scallions, sliced

6 slices bacon, fried and crumbled

2 teaspoons lemon juice

Combine ingredients. Place in au gratin dish or similar container. Microwave for 3-5 minutes on medium-high until hot and bubbly. Serve with crackers or party ryes. Serves 8-10.

Susan Stevens

Hot Stuffed Mushrooms

30 mushrooms

2 tablespoons bleu cheese

3 tablespoons butter

1 cup finely chopped celery

Garlic salt, to taste

Onion salt, to taste

Remove stems and insides of mushrooms. Chop together finely. Combine with remaining ingredients and simmer for 20 minutes. Stuff mushroom caps with mixture. Bake at 375° for 15 minutes. This may be prepared ahead, refrigerated and baked just before serving. Serves 10.

Lynda Goldie

Irresistible Salmon Mousse

2 envelopes unflavored gelatin
1/2 cup water
1 (151/2 ounce) can red salmon
1 cup mayonnaise
1 tablespoon vinegar
Dash of cayenne pepper
2 tablespoons ketchup
Dash of pepper
15 pimiento stuffed olives, sliced
2 hard-cooked eggs, chopped
2 tablespoons sweet pickle relish
1 cup whipping cream, whipped
Lettuce

Combine gelatin and water in small saucepan. Place over medium heat until gelatin is dissolved, stirring constantly. Remove from heat and set aside. Drain salmon and remove skin and bones. Flake salmon with a fork. Add mayonnaise, vinegar, ketchup, cayenne and pepper. Mix well; then stir in olives, eggs, relish and dissolved gelatin. Fold in whipping cream. Spoon mixture into a well-greased 51/2 cup mold. Chill overnight. Unmold on lettuce. If desired, garnish with lemon halves dipped in paprika and topped with parsley sprigs. Yields 1 (51/2 cup) mousse.

Beverley McHugh

Joanne's Cheese Balls

1 (4 ounce) package bleu cheese, crumbled

1 stick butter

1 (8 ounce) package cream cheese, softened

1 (3 ounce) can chopped ripe olives, well-drained

1 bunch green onion tops, chopped

Cream butter and cheeses. Mix with olives and onion tops. Form into a ball, then chill. Serve with bland crackers. Makes 1 large ball.

Joanne Rainey Slaughter

Liver Paté

4 peppercorns

1 teaspoon celery salt

6 cups water

1 pound chicken livers

1/2 pound butter

2 teaspoons dry mustard

1/4 teaspoon nutmeg

1/4 teaspoon ground cloves

1/4 chopped onion

1 clove garlic

1/4 cup port wine

1/2 cup currants

Add peppercorns and celery salt to water and bring to a boil. Add livers and simmer 10 minutes. Drain and discard peppercorns. Place livers in a food processor and add remaining ingredients except currants. Blend until very smooth and turn into crock or bowl. Stir in currants. Cover and refrigerate at least 4 hours. Bring to room temperature before serving. Makes 3 cups. Serves 10-12 slices and 20+ as a spread.

Kay Wing

May be sliced as appetizer or spread as an hors d'oeuvre.

Lou's Shrimp Dip

1 pound cooked shrimp, deveined and chopped
1 (8 ounce) package cream cheese, softened
1/3 cup mayonnaise
3 tablespoons chili sauce
2 tablespoons lemon juice
1 tablespoon onion, minced
1/4 tablespoon Worcestershire
Pinch of sugar

Mix all ingredients. Serve with crackers. Serves 8.

Janet Flowers

Mama's Crab Mornay

An elegant addition to a cocktail buffet.

1 stick butter
2 tablespoons flour
1 pint light cream
1/2 pound Swiss cheese, grated
1 small bunch green onions
1/2 cup chopped parsley
1 tablespoon vermouth
Salt and red pepper to taste
1 pound lump crabmeat

Melt butter in heavy pot. Blend in flour, cream and cheese. Stir until cheese is melted. Add other ingredients. Fold in crabmeat. Serve hot. May be served in chafing dish with melba toast. Serves 12.

Janet Flowers

Mexican Layered Dip

1 (31 ounce) can refried
    beans
11/2 pints sour cream
11/2 (16 ounce) jars picante
    sauce, medium
2 (41/4 ounce) cans black
    olives, chopped
4 tomatoes, chopped

2 bunches green onions,
    chopped
4 small or 2 large ripe
    avocados, chopped
8 ounces shredded cheddar
    cheese
2 large bags tortilla chips

Layer ingredients in order as listed above. Use a
12"x18" serving platter or something similar. Serve
with tortilla chips. Recipe can be cut in half. Serves 24.

Judie Grossman

Mushrooms Trifolati

1 pound mushrooms
3 tablespoons oil
1 garlic clove
4 anchovy filets, crushed

2 tablespoons minced parsley
2 tablespoons lemon juice
Garlic oil

Trim ends of stems from mushrooms. Wash and dry
well. Slice stem and caps thinly. Heat oil in heavy skillet with garlic. When garlic is brown, remove and add
mushrooms. Cook on high heat, stirring often. After 5
minutes, there will be mushroom liquid in pan. Stir a
few tablespoons of mushroom juice into crushed
anchovies, making thick paste. Add paste to mushrooms and mix thoroughly. Cook another 5 minutes
until liquid is absorbed. Add lemon juice, minced parsley and toss lightly. Serve on toast rounds that have
been fried in garlic oil. Serves 12.

Cynthia Quick

Olive Crostini

Double this recipe—use what you need—freeze remaining. Bring frozen crostini olive mixture to room temperature. Use when you need an appetizer.

1/2 cup black olives, pitted
1/2 cup green olives with pimiento
2 medium cloves garlic
1/2 cup Parmesan, grated
4 tablespoons butter
2 tablespoons olive oil
1/2 cup Monterey Jack cheese, grated
1/4 cup fresh parsley, chopped
1 baguette

Preheat oven to broil. Chop olives coarsely in food processor. Transfer to a medium bowl. With machine running, drop garlic through the feed tub of food processor and mince. Add Parmesan, butter and olive oil. Fold in Monterey Jack and parsley. Mix well. Cut baguette into thin slices. Spread each slice to the edges with olive mixture. Cook under broiler until bubbly and lightly browned. Serves 8.

Dottie Gerrity

Paté En Gelér

Unmolds nicely when you run a knife around edge of pan. This recipe can be distributed into two smaller rectangular containers.

1 can beef bouillon
2 packages unflavored gelatin
1 can Sells liver paté
2 (3 ounce) packages cream cheese, softened
Worcestershire to taste

Combine bouillon and gelatin. Heat until gelatin is dissolved, stirring constantly. Place 1/3 of mixture into small rectangular pan and chill until firm. Mix cream cheese, Sells liver paté, Worcestershire sauce and remainder of bouillon in blender. Pour over firm bouillon. Put into refrigerator to set. Ready to serve in about 4 hours or overnight. Serve with any type of crackers. Serves 6-8.

Ellie Loumos

Pesto Dip

2 tablespoons pesto
1 cup low-fat cottage cheese
1 cup light sour cream
1/2 cup aged Parmesan
    cheese, cut into small cubes
1 head red cabbage

Place all ingredients except cabbage into food processor. Process until smooth, then chill. To serve, hollow out interior of cabbage and spoon into cavity. Serve with breadsticks or veggies. Makes 2 cups.

Weezie Windsor

May also be used to fill cherry or grape tomatoes for an appetizer.

Reuben Dip

1 cup mayonnaise (not Miracle
    Whip)
1 (16 ounce) can or jar
    sauerkraut, drained, rinsed
    and squeeze dried
1/4 cup onion, minced
4 (21/2 ounce) packages dried
    corned beef
2 cups Swiss cheese, shredded
1 teaspoon horseradish

Mix all ingredients and bake in 11/2 quart casserole for 30-35 minutes in a 350° preheated oven. Serve hot on party rye bread or Triscuits. Makes about 1 quart. Serves 18-20.

Mary McCarthy

Sausage Stars

2 cups (1 pound) cooked, crumbled sausage
11/2 cups grated sharp cheddar cheese
11/2 cups grated Monterey Jack cheese
1 cup Hidden Valley ranch original salad dressing
1 can (2.25 ounces) sliced ripe olives
1/2 cup chopped red pepper
1 package fresh or frozen wonton wrappers
Vegetable oil

Preheat oven to 350°. Blot sausage dry with paper towels and combine with cheese, salad dressing, olives and red pepper. Lightly grease a mini or regular muffin tin and press 1 wonton wrapper in each cup. Brush with oil. Bake for 5 minutes until golden. Remove from tins and place on baking sheet. Fill with sausage mixture. Bake for 5 minutes until bubbly. Makes 4-5 dozen.

Joan Lee

Shrimp Dip

1 small sweet onion, grated
Small amount of lemon juice
Garlic powder to taste
2 cups fresh shrimp, chopped
1 stick melted butter
1 (8 ounce) package cream cheese, softened
Pinch of salt
4 tablespoons mayonnaise

Mix in order given. Can be frozen. Serves 10-12.

Ruth McNeal

Spiced Nuts

1 tablespoon egg white

2 cups pecans

1/4 cup sugar

1 tablespoon cinnamon

Heat oven to 300°. Mix egg white and pecans until sticky and coated. Mix sugar and cinnamon. Sprinkle over pecans, stirring until coated. Spread on ungreased cookie sheet. Bake for 20 minutes. Recipe can be doubled using 1 pound pecans and 1 egg white. Makes 2 cups.

Irma Dralle-Meyer

Spinach Balls

1 medium onion, diced

2 packages frozen chopped spinach, thawed

2 beaten eggs

3/4 cup melted butter

2 cups Pepperidge Farm stuffing mix

1/2 cup Parmesan cheese

3/4 teaspoon pepper

1/2 teaspoon thyme

1 teaspoon garlic powder

Drain spinach and squeeze dry. Mix all ingredients together. Shape into small balls and place on cookie sheet. Bake at 325° for 25 minutes. Serves 8-24.

Louise Warshauer

Spinach Cheese Mini Muffins

1 (10 ounce) package frozen spinach, thawed and drained well

1 cup small curd cottage cheese (2%)

1 cup egg substitute or 4 eggs, beaten

6 tablespoons mild cheddar cheese, grated

3 tablespoons flour

1 teaspoon garlic powder

1/8 teaspoon salt and freshly ground pepper, to taste

Preheat oven to 350°. Mix all ingredients together. Fill 2 mini muffin, non-stick pans with mixture, stirring often to distribute egg. Bake until tops are golden brown, approximately 30-35 minutes. Remove from oven. Within 5 minutes turn baking pan upside down onto wire rack to remove muffins. Cool on rack. Serve hot or warm. Muffins can be reheated. Makes 24 bite-size muffins.

Phyllis Liebman

Spinach Crostini

1 (10 ounce) package frozen chopped spinach, thawed and drained

2 plum tomatoes, diced

1 garlic clove, minced

1/2 cup crumbled feta cheese

1/4 cup mayonnaise

1/4 cup sour cream

1/2 teaspoon pepper

1 (16 ounce) French bread, cut into 1/2-inch slices

Combine first 7 ingredients. Spread on 1 side of each bread slice. Place on baking sheet. Bake at 350° for 18 minutes or until golden. Serves 10-12.

Ann Ptacek

Tomato, Onion & Anchovy Tart

2 prepared pie crusts

2 pounds Vidalia onions, sliced thin

1/4 cup olive oil

1 (28-32 ounce) can chopped tomatoes

2 small garlic cloves, minced (optional)

1 teaspoon dried thyme, crumbled

1 teaspoon dried rosemary, crumbled

3 tablespoons dry bread crumbs

1/4 cup grated Parmesan

2 (2 ounce) cans flat anchovy filets, drained

Pitted kalamata olives

Fit pie crust into 15"x10"x1" jelly roll pan. Crimp edge, then prick crust with fork; chill. Cook onions in olive oil. Cover with lid over low heat, stirring occasionally for 30 minutes. Add tomatoes, garlic, thyme, rosemary, salt and pepper to taste. Cook mixture uncovered over medium/high heat, stirring for 12 minutes, or until liquid evaporates. Let cool. Preheat oven to 425°. Sprinkle bread crumbs in bottom of crust. Spread mixture evenly over crust and sprinkle with Parmesan. Arrange anchovy filets in diamond pattern over mixture. Place olive in center of each diamond. Bake for 40 minutes. Crust should be golden brown. Cut into squares. Serves 15.

Leslie Branda

Tomato Tart

1 unbaked pie shell

11/2 cups shredded mozzarella cheese

1/4 cup grated fresh Parmesan cheese

4 roma tomatoes or small regular tomatoes

3/4 cup fresh basil leaves

4 cloves of garlic

1/2 cup mayonnaise

1/8 teaspoon white pepper

Unfold crust and place in tart pan or pie pan. Do not prick. Partially bake at 450° for 5-7 minutes, until slightly dry. Remove from oven and sprinkle 1/2 cup mozzarella cheese, then cool in pan on wire rack. Meanwhile, cut tomatoes into slices. Arrange over melted cheese in pan. In food processor combine basil and garlic until coarsely chopped (or snip basil and mince garlic). In medium bowl, combine basil, garlic, and remaining mozzarella, mayonnaise, Parmesan and pepper and spread over tomato slices. Bake at 375° for 20-25 minutes. Let stand 5 minutes before cutting. Serve warm. Makes 8-10 appetizers.

Patricia Weck

Tortilla Roll-ups

8 ounces cream cheese, softened
8 ounces sour cream
1/2 teaspoon seasoned salt
1/2 teaspoon garlic salt or powder
4 ounces chopped ripe olives
4-5 green onions, chopped fine
1/2 cup green or red pepper, chopped fine
1 cup shredded cheddar cheese
10 large tortillas

Mix above ingredients together. Spread evenly onto tortillas. Roll each tortilla up tightly and wrap individually in saran or plastic wrap. Chill in refrigerator several hours. Slice into 1/4-1/2 inch pieces just before serving and place on plate. Serve with picante sauce. Serves 8-24.

Patricia Weck

Zucchini Appetizer

3 cups thinly sliced zucchini
1 cup Bisquick
1/2 cup grated Parmesan cheese
1/2 cup finely chopped onion
2 tablespoons snipped parsley
1/2 teaspoon salt
1/2 teaspoon dried oregano leaves
Dash of pepper
1/2 cup vegetable oil
1 clove garlic, finely chopped
4 eggs, slightly beaten

Heat oven to 350°. Grease 9"x13" pan for appetizer, 81/2"x11" pan for a side dish. Mix all ingredients and spread in pan. Bake until golden brown, about 25 minutes. Freezes well. Makes 40.

Judi Palay

drinks

Bourbon Slush

6 tea bags
7 cups water
1 cup sugar
1 (12 ounce) can frozen
orange juice

1 (6 ounce) can frozen
lemonade
2 cups bourbon

Brew tea. Be sure it is very strong. Dissolve sugar in hot tea. In a large plastic container with a lid mix all ingredients well. Place in freezer. When ready to serve use an ice cream scoop to fill short glasses. Serve with a straw spoon. Serves 20.

Naomi Morris

Brandy Slush

May use 5 teaspoons Sweet'n'Low in place of sugar.

7 cups water
1 1/4 cups sugar
2 cups water
4 tea bags
1 (12 ounce) can orange juice
concentrate

1 (12 ounce) can lemonade
concentrate
2 cups fruit brandy

Dissolve sugar in 7 cups water in a large freezer container. Place tea bags in 2 cups water and bring to a boil. Remove tea bags and add to sugar mix. Add concentrated juices and brandy. Place in freezer. After 12 hours stir to slushy consistency. Return to freezer and leave until frozen, about 24 hours, stirring occasionally. To serve, mix in large glass, 1/2 slush and 1/2 ginger ale. Serves 12-18.

Marjorie White

The Art of Cooking • Hors d'oeuvres & Drinks

Low-cal Fruit Shake

1/2 cup orange juice
1/2 ripe banana
1/2 peach, 1/2 apple, or 5
   strawberries
1 tablespoon plain yogurt

1/4 teaspoon cinnamon
1 teaspoon honey or 1
   package sugar substitute
4-5 ice cubes

In food processor or blender combine all ingredients. Blend on high for 20-30 seconds. Start and stop machine a few times to settle ice. Blend until ice lumps disappear. Serve immediately. May substitute any ripe fruit for fruits above. Makes 1 tall glass.

Joyce Kelly

Mango Daiquiri

10 ice cubes
1 cup chopped mango
1/3 cup fresh lime juice

1/4 cup dark rum
3 tablespoons honey

Put above ingredients in a blender and blend until mixture is smooth and thick, then taste. Add more honey if needed. Makes 2 drinks.

Sally Lopez

Pineapple Mint Frappé

2 (13 1/2 ounce) cans frozen
  pineapple chunks
1/4 cup crème de menthe

1/2 cup coconut
1/4 cup whipping cream
Dash of green food coloring

Thaw 2 cans of pineapple chunks just until contents may be separated. Reserve 1/2 can for garnish. Put remaining pineapple and 1/4 cup crème de menthe in blender. Blend until mixture is frothy and light. Pour into pan and freeze for 30 minutes to 2 hours. Toast coconut in 350° oven for 10 minutes. Whip cream; tint delicate green. Scoop frozen mixture into sherbets and top with reserved pineapple, sprinkling of coconut and swirl of whipped cream. Serves 6.

Elizabeth Griffin

Wassail

Scents the
home
beautifully!

1 1/2 cups sugar
4 cups boiling water
6 whole cloves
1 teaspoon ground ginger

1 (1 inch) stick cinnamon
1 1/2 cups orange juice
1 cup lemon juice

Combine sugar and 2 cups boiling water and boil for 5 minutes. Add spices, cover and let stand 1 hour. Add remaining water and fruit juices. Mix well. Heat to boiling point. Serve immediately. Makes 1 quart.

Marjorie White

White Sangria

3 quarts chablis wine

3/4 cup curacao

1/2 cup brandy

10 ounces frozen strawberries, thawed

10 ounces frozen mixed fruit, thawed

2 oranges, quartered

1 lime, quartered

1 lemon, quartered

Sugar to taste

Fresh fruit to garnish

Combine all ingredients except fresh fruit. Stir until sugar dissolves. Refrigerate 24 hours. Garnish with fresh fruit in serving pitcher. Makes 4 quarts.

Joyce Kelly

notes and recipes

Soups

Apple Soup
Avocado Gazpacho
Big Al's Famous Clam Chili
Blender Gazpacho
Broccoli Potato Soup
Carrot Ginger Soup with Curry
Cauliflower Cheese Soup
Chicken Cheese Soup
Chilled Corn Soup
Cream of Avocado Soup
Cream of Broccoli Soup
Elegant Easy Crab Bisque
Hamburger Soup
Hot Tomato Soup
Italian Tomato Bread Soup
Light Mushroom Soup
Mandarin Soup
New England Clam Chowder
Shrimp Bisque
Spring Green Pea Soup
Summer Melon Soup
Sweet Red Pepper Soup
Watercress Soup (Vegetarian)
Zucchini Soup

Salads

Aunt Mary's Lentil Salad
Baby Spinach, Pear & Goat Cheese Salad
Blue Cheese Salad
Cathleen's Shrimp & Macaroni Salad
Celery Seed Dressing
Company's Coming Chicken Salad
Couscous Salad
Crabmeat Salad
Crunchy Pea Salad
Cucumber Salad
Curried Chicken Salad
Fruited Chicken Salad
Gazpacho Aspic
Glorious Dressing
Hawaiian Fruit Salad
Mandarin Orange Salad
Mango, Pear & Spinach Salad
Merry Mermaid's Fruit Salad
Mom's Potato Salad
New Year's Day Salad
Oriental Salad Dressing
Orzo with Dried Cherries
Orzo Salad with Sesame Dressing
Poppy Seed Dressing
Roasted Pear Salad
Salad Elegante
Shrimp & Avocado Salad
Shrimp Mousse Luncheon Salad
Shrimp Orzo Greek Salad
Shrimp & Pasta Salad
Spinach Cranberry Salad
Spinach Salad with Apricot Vinaigrette
Strawberry Overture
Strawberry Salad
Summer Oriental Salad
Teriyaki Chicken & Mango Salad
Tortellini Salad
Tropical Pasta Salad
Tuna Artichoke Salad
Tuna, Sundried Tomato & Fusilli Pasta Salad
Wild Rice Seafood Salad

Apple Soup

3 cooking apples, i.e. Granny Smith
2 onions
5 cups beef consommé
1 cup cream
Curry powder to taste

Peel and core apples; peel onions. Cut both into chunks. Simmer in consommé until soft. Puree. Add cream and curry powder just before serving. Serves 4.

Grace Seitz

Avocado Gazpacho with Chipotle Sour Cream

2 seeded and chopped cucumbers
3 chopped tomatoes
3-4 minced garlic cloves
1 cup chopped red onion
1 chopped bell pepper
1 (46 ounce) can tomato juice
1 large ripe avocado, peeled and diced
2 tablespoons olive oil
2 tablespoons wine vinegar
1 juiced lime
Tabasco, salt and pepper to taste
1 tablespoon canned chipotle
1 cup sour cream

Place first 5 ingredients in food processor. Leave chunky. Add tomato juice, avocado, olive oil, lime juice and vinegar last. Season with Tabasco, salt and pepper to taste. Mix chipotle chiles and sour cream together for the garnish. Sprinkle with croutons if desired. Serves 4-6.

Georgio Lundy

Big Al's Famous Clam Chili

Mussels or oysters may be substituted for the clams.

1/4 cup olive oil

1 1/4-1 1/3 pounds hot Italian sausage (casing removed)

1 pound coarsely chopped fresh mushrooms

4 cups sliced onions

1 (28 ounce) can whole peeled Italian tomatoes, undrained

1 bottle white wine

1 cup fresh or bottled clam juice

2 tablespoons fresh basil or 2 teaspoons, dried or crumbled

1 whole garlic bud, minced

1 large bunch parsley, chopped

6 dozen little neck clams, scrubbed

Prepare stock a day before serving, as follows. Heat olive oil in large Dutch oven over medium heat. Add sausage, mushrooms and onion. Cook, stirring frequently and breaking sausage with fork until sausage loses pink color. After 10 minutes, stir in tomatoes and bring mixture to a boil, crushing tomatoes into small pieces. Reduce heat to low and simmer 5 minutes. Pour in half the wine plus all of the clam juice. Bring mixture to a boil. Reduce heat to low, cover and simmer 20 minutes, stirring occasionally. Add basil and garlic. Cook 5 minutes longer. Refrigerate stock overnight. Next day remove excess fat from top. Then transfer stock to large pot. Add remaining wine and bring to a boil. Add parsley and clams. Reduce heat to medium high, cover and simmer until clams open, about 5-10 minutes. Discard any clams that do not open. Clam may be removed from shells before serving. Serves 8-10.

Alan Hallene

Blender Gazpacho

2 cups tomato juice

1 cup peeled and chopped tomatoes

1/2 cup finely chopped green pepper

1/2 cup finely chopped celery

1/4 cup finely chopped onion

2 tablespoons fresh parsley

1 clove garlic, minced

2 or 3 tablespoons wine vinegar

2 tablespoons olive oil

1 teaspoon salt

1/2 teaspoon Worcestershire sauce

1/4 teaspoon pepper

Blend all ingredients together in blender. Chill until ready to serve. Serves 8.

Polly Sauder

Broccoli Potato Soup

5-6 potatoes

2 large onions, chopped

4 cloves garlic, chopped

1 cup celery, chopped

3 cups broccoli, chopped

8 cups chicken broth

8 cups shredded cheddar cheese

1 cup milk or cream (optional)

Salt and pepper to taste

Peel and chop potatoes into large diced pieces. Place potatoes, onion, garlic, celery and broccoli into 3-quart saucepan. Add chicken broth and simmer until potatoes are tender—about 40-45 minutes. Cool slightly. Puree in batches using blender or food processor. Return to pan, add cheese and stir until melted. Optional: Add milk or cream until blended. Season to taste. Serves 8-10.

Beverly McGeary

This recipe is a favorite from "The Russian Tea Room" in New York City. It was created by one chef to raise the "dignity" of the lowly potato!!

Carrot Ginger Soup with Curry

Keeps well in refrigerator.

2 tablespoons canola oil
1 large onion, chopped
1/4 cup ginger, chopped fine
2 cloves garlic, minced
1/2 teaspoon curry powder
6 cans chicken broth, unsalted

1 cup dry white wine
11/2-2 pounds carrots, peeled
   and cut into 1/2 inch pieces
1/2 lemon, juice only
1/2 cup plain yogurt or low
   fat sour cream

In large stockpot, over medium heat, sauté first 5 ingredients until soft (not browned), about 15 minutes. Add chicken broth, wine and carrots. Cook uncovered until tender, about 45 minutes over medium heat. Let cool. Puree in blender. Season with lemon juice, salt and pepper to taste. Stir in yogurt or sour cream. Serve hot or cold with a dollop of sour cream and grated carrots or chives for garnish if desired. Serves 6-8.

Edith Alberts

Cauliflower Cheese Soup

3/4 cup onions, chopped
2 tablespoons butter
1 pound cauliflower
1/2 pound butter
2 cups all-purpose flour
10 cups milk
2 cups water

1 pound sharp cheddar
   cheese, shredded
2 tablespoons chicken base
3 tablespoons white wine
Seasoned salt
Salt and pepper to taste

Sauté onions in 2 tablespoons butter until tender. Steam cauliflower until tender, then separate into small flowerets. Melt 1/2 pound butter, add flour and simmer for 10 minutes. Add milk and water and cook over low heat until cream sauce thickens. Add cheese, chicken base, onions, wine, cauliflower, seasoned salt, salt and pepper. Garnish with a sprinkle of paprika and a sprig of parsley, if desired. Serves 12.

Jane Borchers

Chicken Cheese Soup

1/4 cup margarine
1/2 cup celery, chopped
1/2 cup onion, chopped
1/4 cup flour

4 cups evaporated milk
8 ounces Port Wine cheese
3 cups diced cooked chicken
Salt, pepper and chives

Melt margarine. Sauté celery and onion until soft. Stir in flour, then stir in milk. Add cheese and stir in until melted. Add chicken and heat. Add salt and pepper to taste. Serve topped with chives. Serves 6.

Kay Wing

Chilled Corn Soup

I have made corn soup with fresh corn, but I didn't feel there was enough of a corn taste.

4 cans creamed corn
1/4 cup unsalted butter
1/3 cup minced shallots
11/2 cups water
1/4 cup dry white wine

1/2 cup Half and Half
Salt, white pepper
Fresh chopped chives
White truffle oil

Pour creamed corn into a separate bowl. Set aside. Melt butter in heavy saucepan over medium heat. Sauté shallots until tender, about 3 minutes. Add corn, water and wine. Bring to a boil. Simmer for 2 minutes. Cool 10 minutes. Puree soup in batches in blender. Strain by forcing through sieve. Cool and add Half and Half. Season with salt and white pepper. Chill at least 5 hours. Serve with chopped fresh chives and drizzled truffle oil on top. Serves 6.

Val Wright

Cream of Avocado Soup

3 ripe medium avocados
2 thin slices of onion
1 cup chicken stock

1/3 cup sour cream
1/2 cup heavy cream
2 tablespoons lemon juice

Puree all ingredients. Serve cold, garnished with sour cream and paprika. May be thinned, if desired, with stock or cream. Lowfat yogurt can be substituted for heavy cream. Serves 2-4.

Sue White

Cream of Broccoli Soup

2 chicken bouillon cubes
1 1/2 cups water
3 tablespoons melted butter
3 tablespoons flour
2 cups milk

9 ounces chopped fresh broccoli
1 cup cubed Velveeta cheese
Salt and pepper to taste

Boil water and cubes for 5 minutes. Mix melted butter and flour together in 2-quart pan. Add milk and boil gently until thick and creamy. Boil broccoli for 10 minutes and puree in blender. Add to milk mixture. Add cubed cheese and salt and pepper to taste. Serves 4.

Irma Dralle-Meyer

Elegant Easy Crab Bisque

1/4 cup olive oil
1 package seasoning mix (frozen onions, peppers and celery)
1 jar prepared tomato-basil sauce
1 jar alfredo sauce

1 (14 ounce) can chicken broth
2 cans crabmeat
1/2 cup dry sherry, heated
Sour cream
Shallots, cut up

For added elegance add a dollop of sour cream with shallots on top when you serve.

Sauté frozen vegetables in large saucepan in oil. Add jars of both sauces and chicken broth. Then add crab and cook for 20 minutes. Serve with heated sherry. Pour 1 ounce in bowl when serving. Serves 6.

Char Macaluso

Hamburger Soup

As it is with most soups—it gets better than ever the next day.

1 1/2 pounds ground chuck beef
1 cup chopped onion
1 cup chopped celery
1 cup chopped carrots
1 cup chopped green pepper
2 cups chopped cabbage
1 (28 ounce) can crushed tomatoes
1 tablespoon Better than Bouillon chicken base
1 tablespoon Better than Bouillon beef base
2 quarts water
2 teaspoons dill
2 teaspoons Worcestershire
1 teaspoon salt
1/2 teaspoon pepper

Brown the beef and onions; put all of the ingredients into a soup pot and simmer for several hours. Serves 6-8.

Terry Terrill

Hot Tomato Soup

2 tablespoons olive oil
1 cup diced sweet onion
6 fresh basil leaves
Salt and fresh ground pepper to taste
2 1/2 pounds (5 cups) fresh tomatoes, seeded
1/4 cup finely chopped celery
4 cups fresh chicken stock
1 teaspoon sugar (optional)
1/2 cup goat cheese
1/4 cup flour

Heat olive oil, onions, chopped basil leaves, salt and pepper. Cook, stirring until onions are wilted. Add tomatoes, chopped celery and stir to blend with flour and crumbled goat cheese. Simmer for 10 minutes (make sure it does not stick or scorch). Add broth and heat thoroughly. Serve by topping each bowl with a dab of sour cream and a basil leaf. Serves 8.

Myra Janco Daniels

Italian Tomato Bread Soup

1/2 cup extra virgin olive oil
1 pound mild Italian sausage
3 cloves chopped garlic
1/2 cup fresh sage leaves
8 ounces or 1 baguette of
   dense Italian bread

Salt
Fresh ground pepper
2 (28 ounce) cans of good
   quality chopped (skinless)
   tomatoes
8 cups chicken stock

In heavy stockpot, cook sliced sausage in olive oil over medium heat until browned. Remove with a slotted spoon to a paper towel and drain. Add garlic and sage; cook until the garlic turns a light golden color. Thinly slice the entire baguette and add to seasoned oil. Brown the bread on both sides and season with salt and pepper. While the bread is browning, in a separate pot, bring the chicken stock to a boil.

Drain tomatoes, reserving the juice. Add tomatoes to the browned bread and stir with a wooden spoon over high heat for 2 minutes. Pour in the chicken stock, reduce heat and simmer 1 hour. Add sausage in the last 10 minutes of cooking. Adjust seasoning and add reserved tomato juice if desired. Garnish with Italian parsley. Serves 6.

Sandra Figge

Serve with a crisp green salad, topped with lemon vinaigrette dressing for a light and delicious Italian dinner.

Light Mushroom Soup

Preparation time is about 15 minutes and cooking time is 20 minutes.

1 large onion
1 small garlic clove
1/2 large bell pepper
2 tablespoons butter or margarine
1/2 pound mushrooms

2 tablespoons flour
2 cups chicken or vegetable broth
2/3 cup milk
Salt and pepper to taste
1-2 twigs of parsley

Remove the skin of onion and garlic, wash the bell pepper and dry, removing the seeds and white membrane separating the walls. Chop all 3 items. Melt butter at low temperature and simmer onion, garlic and bell pepper for 5 minutes. Clean and wash mushrooms, then slice and add to the above 3 items. Simmer for another 3 minutes until fully cooked. Spread flour and mix well with the mushrooms. Add chicken broth (or vegetable) and boil over high heat. While stirring, cook for 5 minutes until soup is slightly thickened. Reduce heat and add milk. Season well with salt and pepper and bring the soup once more to a boil. In the meantime, wash parsley, dry, chop and mix into soup. Fill the mushroom soup into 4 soup bowls and serve at once. Serves 4.

Ernest & Nancy Furstner

Mandarin Soup

1/2 pound raw lean pork, ground

1 package frozen, chopped spinach

6 cups bouillon (beef or chicken)

1/2 cup shredded carrots

2 tablespoons cornstarch

3 tablespoons water

1 tablespoon soy sauce

1/2 teaspoon salt

1 egg

Sauté pork. Cook spinach in bouillon. Add carrots. Make a paste with the 2 tablespoons cornstarch and 3 tablespoons water. Add paste, soy sauce, salt and pork to spinach and warm until it thickens to soup consistency. Just before serving, beat 1 egg and add slowly to hot mixture, stirring constantly. Egg curdles, but will be appetizing. Serves 6.

Suzie Lipp

New England Clam Chowder

Quick and
low budget.

1/2 stick butter
1/2 diced onion
1 small bottle clam juice
5 potatoes peeled and diced
5 cans baby clams
1 1/2 quarts, Half and Half
cream

Cornstarch or potato flakes to
thicken, as necessary
Salt and pepper to taste
5 shots Worcestershire sauce
5 shots Tabasco

Melt butter and sauté onion in clam juice. Add potatoes, cook approximately 10 minutes. Add clams from can with juice and then add Half and Half, slowly stirring. Thicken, as necessary with cornstarch or potato flakes. A slight bit of water may be added to same. Salt, pepper, Worcestershire and Tabasco to taste. Garnish with slice of butter and paprika. Serves 4-6.

Joe Batchelder

Shrimp Bisque

8 ounces cream cheese
2 cups skim milk
1 can chicken broth
2 cans cream of celery soup
1 can zesty tomato soup
1/2 cup dry sherry
1 teaspoon lemon juice

1 pound shrimp, cooked and
diced
3 green onions, minced
2 tablespoons fresh dill
1 tomato, seeded and chopped
Parsley, chopped

Serve in bread bowls for a spectacular presentation!

In a large saucepan, blend cream cheese and milk.
Add chicken broth, celery soup and tomato soup.
Whisk ingredients and add sherry and lemon juice.
Add shrimp, onions, dill and tomato. Refrigerate
until ready to serve. Do not boil. Garnish with pars-
ley. Makes 10 cups.

Joanne Rainey Slaughter

Spring Green Pea Soup

1 package frozen peas
1 cup skim or homogenized
milk
1 cup chicken broth
1 tablespoon dill weed
1 teaspoon sugar

1 tablespoon butter (optional)
1/4 teaspoon white pepper
(optional)
Fresh dill and dollop of sour
cream for garnish (optional)

Cook peas in microwave or according to package
directions. Combine all ingredients in a blender.
Serve warm or cold. Serves 4.

Pam Weston

Summer Melon Soup

1/2 cup pureed honeydew
1 cup pureed cantaloupe
1/2 cup pureed peeled and
   seeded cucumber
1 cup plain yogurt
3/4 cup light cream

1/2 teaspoon celery salt
11/2 teaspoon minced parsley
1/2 cup chopped honeydew
1/2 cup chopped cantaloupe
1/2 cup chopped cucumber

Blend first 7 ingredients. Chill at least 2 hours. Stir in last 3 ingredients. Serves 4.

Paul George

Sweet Red Pepper Soup

1/4 cup olive oil
3 shallots, chopped
4 carrots, chopped
2 pears, cored and chopped
2 (14 ounce) cans chicken
   broth

8 large sweet red peppers,
   chopped
1 tablespoon hot red pepper
   flakes
Salt to taste
Sour cream to garnish

Heat oil. Add all ingredients except chicken broth. Sauté for 10 minutes, then add chicken broth. Simmer for 20 minutes, then puree in food processor and return to pan. Add red pepper flakes and salt. Heat well. Serve in soup bowls garnished with sour cream. Serves 6.

Char Macaluso

Watercress Soup (Vegetarian)

2 bunches of watercress
1 white onion, diced
2 white potatoes, peeled, diced and cooked
5 cups vegetable broth, canned

Salt to taste
1/2 teaspoon nutmeg
1 cup Half and Half
Sour cream or crème fraiche

Remove large stems from watercress, rinse and drain. Reserve small sprigs or leaves for garnish. Sauté onion, add watercress and potato. Add 1/2 of the broth. Add salt and nutmeg. Add Half and Half and heat until warm; do not boil. Blend. Add remaining broth. Garnish with sour cream or crème fraiche. Serves 6.

Shirley Chosy

Zucchini Soup

2 pounds zucchini, thinly sliced
2 shallots, chopped
4 tablespoons butter

1/2 cup water
1 teaspoon curry powder
1/8 teaspoon garlic powder
2 cans chicken broth

Sauté zucchini and shallots slowly in butter (zucchini should not be peeled). Add spices and water and cook until zucchini becomes wilted. Stir frequently. Do not brown. Puree in blender until completely smooth. Add broth and taste for seasoning. May be served hot or cold. Serves 4.

Grace Seitz

Aunt Mary's
Lentil Salad

1 pound dried lentils, cooked and drained

1 bunch parsley, chopped

7 ribs and leaves of celery, chopped

3 large tomatoes, chopped

1 bunch scallions, chopped

1/2 bunch dill, chopped (optional)

1 cup extra virgin olive oil

1/2 cup white vinegar

Dash Tabasco sauce

Garlic crushed, to taste

Salt and pepper to taste

1 tablespoon chopped mint (optional)

Cook lentils in boiling salted water, approximately 25 minutes until tender. Let cool while chopping other ingredients. Combine in a large bowl and mix. Garnish with tomato slices. Serves 20.

Mary Injaian

Baby Spinach, Pear & Goat Cheese Salad

3 firm, ripe pears

Juice of 1 small lemon

8 cups baby spinach leaves

1/2 cup pitted sweet dried
cherries

1/3 cup olive oil

2 tablespoons sherry vinegar

1/2 teaspoon salt and freshly
ground pepper to taste

4-5 ounces goat cheese, cut
into small pieces

Peel, halve and core pears. Cut each in half and into 4 wedges. Place in large bowl and sprinkle with lemon juice. Add spinach and cherries. For the dressing, whisk together olive oil, vinegar, salt and pepper. Add dressing to salad; toss well. Top salad with goat cheese. Serves 6.

Nina Foster

Blue Cheese Salad

To make a light lunch dish, add chicken breast or slice 2-3 ripe pears and add toasted walnuts.

4 tablespoons crumbled blue cheese

2 tablespoons freshly grated Parmesan cheese

2 cloves pressed garlic

Olive oil

1 bunch green onions, sliced and omit green tops

1 large green leaf lettuce, torn into bite-size bits

1 lemon

Salt and pepper

Put blue cheese, Parmesan and garlic in a large salad bowl. Add enough olive oil to make a thin paste, mashing ingredients with a fork. Add green onions and lettuce. Let sit on top of cheese paste for 20-30 minutes at room temperature. Squeeze half of a lemon onto lettuce. Toss. Season to taste with salt and pepper. Add more lemon juice if desired. Serves 4-6.

Joann Duncan

Cathleen's Shrimp & Macaroni Salad

1/2 cup vegetable oil

1/2 cup lemon juice

1 package Italian dressing mix

1 teaspoon horseradish

11/2 cup broccoli florets

1 cup shredded carrots

11/2 cup sliced zucchini

1/4 cup chopped green onion

2 cups uncooked macaroni, cooked and drained

4 ounces fresh cooked shrimp

Add oil, lemon juice, salad dressing mix and horseradish to a cruet and shake. Combine vegetables with macaroni and shrimp. Toss with dressing. Cover and chill several hours or overnight before serving. Serves 6-8.

Suzanne Payne

Celery Seed Dressing

1 cup sugar

2 tablespoons celery seed

1 teaspoon salt

1 cup mayonnaise

1 cup cider vinegar

1 tablespoon minced garlic

1 tablespoon Dijon mustard

2 cups vegetable oil

Red onion

Walnuts

Dried cherries

Salad greens

Mix together all ingredients. Drizzle some oil onto greens. Garnish with sliced red onion and dried cherries. Serves 8.

Nancy Johnston

Company's Coming Chicken Salad

1 (16 ounce) box orzo, cooked

4 cups cooked diced chicken breast

2 cups seedless red grapes, halved

2 cups peeled and diced European cucumber

1 cup chopped celery

3/4 cup toasted pecans

1/2 cup diced cherries

Dressing:

2 cups mayonnaise

1/4 cup Half and Half

2 teaspoons salt

2 tablespoons lemon juice

2 teaspoons white pepper

You can add 3/4 cup chopped baby spinach leaves for color.

Assemble the first 7 ingredients. Mix last 5 ingredients (dressing) and add to the chicken mixture. Assemble at least 2 hours ahead and refrigerate. Serves 10.

Anne Steffen

Couscous Salad

1 box prepared plain couscous
10 ounces fresh spinach,
   slivered
1/2 cup fresh dill, chopped
1 red onion, minced

Lemon Vinaigrette Dressing:
1/4 cup fresh lemon juice
1/2 cup light olive oil
2 cloves garlic, minced
Salt and pepper to taste

Mix dressing. Stir dressing into warm couscous. Chill 4-5 hours or overnight. Before serving, add dill, onion and spinach. Mix and serve. Keeps well for 2 days. Serves 10.

Dottie Gerrity

Crabmeat Salad

21/2 pounds cooked lump
   crabmeat
3 avocados, peeled and cut
   into cubes
1/2 cup finely chopped celery
1/2 cup sliced radishes
1/4 cup lemon juice
1/4 cup vinegar
3 tablespoons olive oil
2 tablespoons chopped green
   onion
1/4 teaspoon cayenne

Salt to taste
1 teaspoon Worcestershire sauce
Bibb lettuce as base

Dressing:
1 cup mayonnaise
1/4 cup chili sauce
2 tablespoons chopped parsley
1 tablespoon chopped onion
1 tablespoon chopped chives
Dash cayenne
1/4 cup heavy cream, whipped

Combine all ingredients. Serve on lettuce-lined plates. To make the dressing, combine all ingredients and chill. Spoon over salad. Serves 6-8.

Roberta Tharpe

Crunchy Pea Salad

2 Birdseye deluxe tiny peas (10 ounce packages)
1 large fresh red pepper
1 cup cauliflower, flowerets only
1 bunch scallions

3/4 cup "original" ranch dressing
1/3 cup sour cream
Salt and pepper to taste
Cold shrimp optional

In advance, thaw and drain peas well. Chop red pepper in cubes. Chop tips of cauliflower florets. Add chopped scallions. Combine sour cream with ranch dressing. Add to salad an hour before serving, but do not put in more than you need or salad will become too liquid. Add cooked, cold, medium-sized shrimp if desired. Serves 6-8.

Maggie Foskett

Cucumber Salad

2 tablespoons white vinegar
2 tablespoons canola oil
4 tablespoons sugar
2 cucumbers, peeled and sliced

1/2 cup Vidalia or sweet onion, cut in slices
Salt and pepper

Mix first 3 ingredients. Add to cucumbers and onion, then add salt and pepper. Mix to coat cucumbers and onion. Refrigerate for at least 4 hours. You can add more vinegar if desired. Serves 2-4.

Sandra Hesse

I prefer using hydroponic cucumbers.

Curried Chicken Salad

Since I like curry, I usually taste and then add more! Depends on how much curry you like.

3/4 cup mayonnaise
1 tablespoon chopped green onion
1 teaspoon curry powder
1/8 teaspoon pepper

2 cups cooked cubed chicken
1/2 cup chopped apple
1/4 cup sliced celery
1/4 cup raisins

In medium bowl, combine mayonnaise, onion, curry powder and pepper. Add chicken, apple, celery and raisins. Toss to coat well. Cover and chill. Serves 4-6.

Lyn Scanlon

Fruited Chicken Salad

Shrimp can be substituted for chicken.

4 cups diced, cooked chicken
1 (15 ounce) can pineapple chunks, drained
1 cup chopped celery
1 (11 ounce) can mandarin orange sections, drained
1/2 cup sliced, pitted ripe olives
1/2 cup chopped green pepper

2 tablespoons grated onion
1 cup mayonnaise or salad dressing
1 tablespoon prepared mustard
1 (5 ounce) can chow mein noodles
Lettuce leaves

In a large bowl combine cooked chicken, pineapple, celery, oranges, olives, green pepper and onion. Blend mayonnaise or salad dressing and mustard. Toss gently with chicken mixture. Cover and chill several hours. Just before serving, mix in chow mein noodles. Serve in lettuce-lined serving bowl. Serves 8.

Judie Grossman

Gazpacho Aspic

2 packs gelatin
3 cups V-8 juice
1/4 cup wine vinegar
1 clove garlic, crushed
2 teaspoons salt
1/4 teaspoon pepper
Dash of cayenne pepper
1/2 cup chopped celery

1/2 cup chopped green pepper
1/2 cup chopped cucumber
1/2 teaspoon cumin, ground

Topping:
1/2 cup sour cream
1/3 cup mayonnaise
1/2 teaspoon salt

This is easy and a wonderful accompaniment to fish entrees or rich stews.

Soften gelatin in 1 cup V-8. Heat until mixture simmers. Add remaining V-8, vinegar, garlic and seasonings. Chill until mixture begins to set (about 45 minutes to an hour). Fold in vegetables and pour into any 6-cup container or mold. Add topping and sprinkle with chives. Serves 6.

Audrey Salb

Glorious Dressing

4 cloves garlic

3 tablespoons chopped onions

1/2 cup vegetable oil

3/4 cup olive oil

1/2 cup red wine vinegar

3 tablespoons water

3 tablespoons sugar

1 1/2 teaspoons basil, dried

1 1/2 teaspoons thyme, dried

1 1/2 teaspoons salt

2 cups aged Parmesan cheese

In a food processor or blender, process garlic and onion. Pour in a slow stream—vegetable and olive oil. Add 1 tablespoon of the vinegar at a time. Add water, sugar and seasonings. Gradually add the cheese. Process until creamy. Refrigerate 2 hours before serving. Will keep in refrigerator for months. Excellent on pasta, green salads, tuna and chicken salads. Makes 2 cups.

Weezie Windsor

Hawaiian Fruit Salad

1 (20 ounce) can pineapple
  tidbits
5 medium firm bananas, halved
  (lengthwise and sliced)
1 (16 ounce) can whole
  cranberry sauce

1/2 cup sugar
1 (12 ounce) carton frozen
  whipped topping, thawed
1/2 cup chopped walnuts

Drain pineapple juice into a medium bowl; set pineapple aside. Add bananas to the juice. In a large bowl, combine cranberry sauce and sugar. Remove bananas, discarding juice, and add to cranberry mixture. Stir in pineapple, whipped topping and nuts. Pour into a 13"x19"x 2" dish. Freeze until solid. Remove from the freezer 15 minutes before cutting. Serves 12-16.

Fran Sisson Downing

Mandarin Orange Salad

Tear up lettuce and sliced onions a day ahead and keep in ziplock bag so lettuce absorbs onion flavor. In separate container, prepare dressing a day ahead as well.

1 large bunch red leaf lettuce
1 bunch green onions
4 ounces slivered almonds
1 small can mandarin oranges, drained
1/4 cup pine nuts
8 strips of bacon, cooked and crumbled

Dressing:
4 tablespoons sugar
2 teaspoons salt
1/2 teaspoon lemon pepper
4 tablespoons balsamic vinegar
1/2 cup salad oil
1/2 teaspoon soy sauce
1 teaspoon Worcestershire sauce

Tear up lettuce into smaller pieces, discarding spine pieces. Slice green onions, using white part and small parts of the green. Mix all ingredients together. Pour dressing over and toss. Serves 10.

Yvonne Locker

Mango, Pear & Spinach Salad

Dressing:

1/8 teaspoon kosher salt

3/4 teaspoon raw garlic, finely chopped

3 tablespoons extra virgin olive oil

2 tablespoons balsamic vinegar

3 tablespoons orange juice

6 ounce bag baby spinach

2 ripe D'Anjou pears, cored and cut into thin slices

3 ounces blue cheese, crumbled

2 ripe mangoes, peeled and chopped into chunks

3/4 cup walnuts, coarsely chopped and then roasted

You can eliminate mangoes if desired.

Wash spinach and cut off stems, if desired. Drain excess water. In a small bowl create dressing by mixing together salt, garlic, oil, balsamic vinegar and orange juice until well blended. Set dressing aside. In serving bowl, mix together spinach, pears and mangoes. Pour dressing slowly until spinach mixture is well coated. Roast walnuts for 5 minutes at 300°. Add blue cheese and walnuts and toss lightly. Serves 6.

Fran Gilbert

Merry Mermaid's Fruit Salad

1/2 watermelon	Marinade:
1 honeydew melon	1 cup sugar
8 peaches	3/4 cup water
1 pineapple	1/4 cup lime juice
1 quart strawberries	1/2-1 cup Cointreau liqueur
1 pint blueberries	Mint leaves to taste

Cut melons into cubes or balls. Slice peaches and pineapple. Add berries. Dissolve sugar in water and boil for 5 minutes. Cool and then add lime juice, liqueur and mint leaves. Pour this mixture over the fruit. Marinate for several hours or overnight. Serves 12.

Jane Borchers

Mom's Potato Salad

5 pounds red potatoes
3 tablespoons cider vinegar
1 tablespoon Lawry's
  seasoned salt
1 tablespoon Lawry's lemon
  pepper
2 tablespoons sugar
1 tablespoon celery seed

1 large green pepper, cut in
  1/4 inch pieces
1 cup mayonnaise, thinned with
  water to pudding consistency
1 small jar pimientos, cut up
4-6 hard cooked eggs, cut
  into small pieces

Boil potatoes until tender (with skins on). Remove from water, let cool, then peel and cut potatoes into chunks. Sprinkle with vinegar and let stand for 15 minutes. Add other ingredients in order given. Mix thoroughly; chill until ready to serve. Serves 12-15.

Joyce Lindsey

New Year's Day Salad

1 head of lettuce, chopped
1 head of cauliflower, florets
1 small red onion, sliced thin
1 pound bacon, cooked and
  crumbled

1 pint Hellmann's mayonnaise
1/2 cup Parmesan cheese
1/4 cup sugar

Layer first 4 ingredients in large bowl. Mix next 3 ingredients together and spread on top. Cover and refrigerate 12 hours. Toss and serve. Serves 12-15.

Linda Meyer

Oriental Salad Dressing

I cup salad oil
I cup honey
1/2 cup rice vinegar

2 teaspoons soy sauce
I teaspoon garlic powder
I teaspoon onion powder

Blend ingredients. Put in glass jar. Makes 2 1/2 cups.

Mary Trier

Orzo with Dried Cherries

I cup orzo
Zest from I orange
Juice of I orange
3 tablespoons olive oil
Salt to taste
1/3 cup dried cherries or
    dried cranberries

2 tablespoons slivered
    almonds, toasted
2 green onions or scallions,
    minced

Bring 6 cups water to a boil with 2 teaspoons salt. Add orzo and cook for 8 minutes or until al dente. Drain. While pasta is cooking, mix juice and zest in a small processor or by hand with a whisk. Add olive oil slowly so dressing emulsifies (thickens and blends oil into juice; looks cloudy). Add salt to taste. Toss cooked, drained pasta with orange juice mixture, dried cherries or cranberries and half of the green onion. Just before serving garnish with remaining green onion and almonds. Serve at room temperature. Serves 4.

Sandra Roth

Orzo Salad with Sesame Dressing

1 pound orzo, uncooked
1 tablespoon sesame oil
4 carrots, cut in strips or
  1 (8 ounce) package carrot
  sticks
2 cups raisins
1 cup sunflower seeds, toasted

2 tablespoons fresh chopped
  parsley
2 tablespoons sliced green
  onions
2/3 cup orange oriental splash
  dressing
1/3 cup sesame oil

Cook orzo in boiling water until tender. Drain and rinse with cold water, then drain again. Combine orzo and 1 tablespoon sesame oil. Toss gently. Spoon half of the orzo in a large glass bowl. Top with half carrots, raisins and sunflower seeds. Repeat layers. Mix last 2 ingredients to make the dressing. Drizzle with 1 cup sesame dressing. Combine chopped parsley and sliced onions. Sprinkle on top. Serves 8-12.

Dorothy Wege

Poppy Seed Dressing

1 cup honey	1 cup salad oil
1/2 cup vinegar	1 teaspoon dry mustard
1/2 medium onion, grated	2 tablespoons poppy seeds

In small saucepan, dissolve honey in vinegar over medium high heat; then cool. Add onion, salad oil, mustard and poppy seeds. Whisk all ingredients together. Chill in glass container. Keeps well in refrigerator. Makes 3-4 cups.

Helen Stephens

Roasted Pear Salad

Do not refrigerate pears after roasting.

4 pounds firm pears	3 tablespoons red wine vinegar
1 tablespoon unsalted butter, melted	Salt and pepper to taste
2 tablespoons sugar	12 cups mixed baby greens
2 cups ruby port	3/4 cup Roquefort cheese
1 shallot, sliced	1 cup candied walnuts or pecans
1 cup olive oil	

Heat oven to 500° with baking sheet on middle rack. Peel, halve and core each pear. Cut halves into fifths. Toss pears into butter. Add sugar and toss again. Placing flat on baking sheet, roast pears until brown on bottom—about 10 minutes. Turn and roast other side until brown. Set aside and prepare dressing. Boil port and shallot in heavy saucepan for 1 minute. Simmer until liquid is reduced to 1/2 cup. Strain. Pour reduction into large salad bowl. Whisk in oil and vinegar. Season with salt and pepper. Add greens, cheese, nuts and pears. Coat. Divide among plates. Serves 8.

Val Wright

Salad Elegante

3 heads Bibb or Boston lettuce
1 can hearts of palm, sliced
1 (14 ounce) can artichoke
   hearts, quartered (not
   marinated)
1/2 pound frozen baby shrimp
   (cooked and chilled)

12 medium mushrooms, sliced
1 small can sliced black olives
1 small jar pimientos
Bottled champagne dressing,
   chilled

Place lettuce on chilled plates. Top the lettuce with hearts of palm, artichokes, shrimp, mushrooms, olives and pimientos. Serve with champagne dressing. Serves 6-8.

Sally Taylor

Shrimp & Avocado Salad

1 cup olive oil
2 pounds shrimp (cooked and
   cleaned)
1 cup onion, chopped
3/4 cup white wine vinegar
1 cup minced celery
1/4 cup undrained capers
7 bay leaves

1 teaspoon salt
1 teaspoon celery seed
1 teaspoon pepper
Dash of hot pepper sauce, to
   taste
2 avocados
Lettuce leaves

Toss first 11 ingredients and chill for 24 hours. Before serving on lettuce leaves, remove bay leaves and add peeled, sliced avocados to shrimp mixture. Serves 6.

Claire Kruchten

Shrimp Mousse Luncheon Salad

2 tablespoons unflavored gelatin
1/4 cup water
1 can condensed tomato soup
8 ounces cream cheese
3/4 cup chopped celery

3/4 cup chopped scallions
2 cans small shrimp (do not
   use fresh or frozen)
1 cup mayonnaise
Lettuce leaves

Soften gelatin in water. Heat unduluted soup to a boil. Dissolve cream cheese in soup. Add gelatin and stir. Cool. Add vegetables, shrimp and mayonnaise. Pour into a 6 cup greased mold or 6 individual greased molds. Chill at least 8 hours. Carefully unmold onto lettuce. Garnish with vegetable sticks if desired. Serves 6.

Beth George

Shrimp Orzo Greek Salad

Vinaigrette Dressing:

1 teaspoon lemon zest

1/4 cup fresh lemon juice

1/2 cup olive oil

1 tablespoon chopped fresh dill

1 teaspoon minced garlic

1/2 teaspoon kosher salt and pepper

16 jumbo raw shrimp, deveined and peeled

1 cup orzo pasta

5 ounces feta cheese, crumbled

3/4 cup chopped red bell pepper

1/3 cup Kalamata olives, chopped

2 tablespoons thinly sliced scallions

1 1/2 tablespoons chopped oregano

Preparation time: 15 minutes. Do not overcook pasta. Can also use curly pasta. Chill before serving.

In a small bowl, whisk together dressing ingredients. Place shrimp in medium bowl with 1/4 cup dressing. Toss to coat shrimp. Cover and chill 30 minutes. Cook orzo until al dente. Drain and place in bowl. Add remaining dressing and feta cheese. Toss well. Add the red bell pepper, olives, scallions and oregano. Thread 4 shrimp each onto 4 skewers, making sure shrimp is bent so it passes through skewer twice. Place shrimp over high heat. Grill 4-5 minutes. Serve grilled shrimp over the orzo mixture. Serves 6.

Dottie Gerrity

Shrimp & Pasta Salad

1 pound shrimp, cleaned and deveined

1/2 package spiral pasta

1/2-1 cup mayonnaise

1/2 cup frozen tiny peas, (pour boiling water over and drain)

1/4 cup minced fresh herbs (basil, dill and parsley)

1/2 cup chopped scallions

4 teaspoons tarragon vinegar, to taste

Dressing:

1/3 cup wine vinegar

1/2 cup sugar

1 cup salad oil

1 teaspoon salt

1/4 cup onion (optional)

1 teaspoon dry mustard

2 tablespoons water

Cook shrimp until pink; cool, then split lengthwise almost through to butterfly. Cook pasta al dente. Mix with shrimp. Add rest of ingredients. Salt and pepper to taste. Garnish with parsley. Make the day before serving. To make the dressing, mix all ingredients together in blender. Serves 4-6.

Mrs. R. Laird

Spinach Cranberry Salad

1 package triple washed baby
  spinach
1 package dried cranberries or
  dried cherries
1/2 cup slivered almonds
2 tablespoons sugar, to
  crystallize almonds
1/2 stick butter

Dressing:
1 tablespoon purple onion
3 tablespoons balsamic vinegar
1/2 cup olive oil
1 1/2 teaspoons mustard
1 teaspoon honey
Salt and pepper to taste

Mix spinach and cranberries or cherries in a large bowl. Melt butter in skillet and add sugar and almonds. Sauté until the almonds are very lightly browned. Remove from heat and allow almonds to cool in the pan. Drain on paper towels. Mix dressing ingredients in Cuisinart or whisk by hand. Combine with spinach mixture and sprinkle crystallized almonds on top. Serves 4-6.

Pauline Hendel

Spinach Salad with Apricot Vinaigrette

1 package (10 ounce) fresh baby spinach
1 pint grape tomatoes, halved
1 small red onion, thinly sliced
1/2 cup chopped dried apricots
1 (4 ounce) package crumbled goat cheese
1 ripe avocado, peeled and diced
1/2 cup chopped pecans, toasted

Apricot Vinaigrette:
1/3 cup vegetable oil
2 tablespoons white wine vinegar
2 tablespoons orange juice
2 tablespoons apricot jam
1/2 teaspoon salt
1/2 teaspoon ground coriander
1/2 teaspoon freshly ground pepper

Place first 7 ingredients in a large bowl, tossing gently. Drizzle with Apricot Vinaigrette, tossing gently to coat. Preparation time: 10 minutes. Serves 6.

Helen Rosenthal

Strawberry Overture

2 small packages strawberry
jello
1 cup boiling water
2 (10 ounce) packages frozen
strawberries, thawed

1 (1 pound 4 ounce) can
crushed pineapple, drained
3 medium bananas, mashed
1 pint sour cream

Excellent
with ham or
tasty enough
to serve as
dessert.

Combine jello and boiling water in large bowl. Stir
in strawberries and juice, pineapple and bananas. Put
1/2 of mixture in 13"x9" glass Pyrex dish and refrigerate until set (11/2 hours). Remove from refrigerator and spread with sour cream. Gently pour balance
of mixture over this and refrigerate. Serves 8-10.

Nancy Porter

Strawberry Salad

1 (10 ounce) package baby
spinach
1 pint strawberries, sliced
1/3 cup crumbled blue cheese
1/3 cup toasted walnuts

Dressing:
1/2 cup sugar
1/2 cup vegetable oil
1/2 cup white wine vinegar
1 tablespoon sesame seeds
1 tablespoon poppy seeds
1/4 teaspoon paprika
1 tablespoon onion, chopped

Blend dressing ingredients in blender. Toss spinach
with dressing; add strawberries, cheese and walnuts.
Serves 8-10.

Nancy Woltz

Summer Oriental Salad

Great for picnics, potlucks or outdoor buffets (no mayo, cream or eggs). Can add 1 pound julienne turkey cubed for main dish.

2 cups raw basmati or Texmati rice

3 1/2 cups water or chicken broth

8 ounces fresh snow peas, washed and strung

1/2 cup thinly sliced green onions

3 medium carrots, peeled and coarsely shredded

2 red bell peppers, coarsely chopped

1 (7 ounce) can sliced water chestnuts, rinsed and drained

1/2 cup chopped fresh cilantro (or parsley)

1/2 cup toasted sliced almonds

Oriental Dressing:

1/3 cup Chinese soy sauce

1/4 cup peanut oil (or vegetable oil)

3 tablespoons sesame oil

1 tablespoon hot and sweet mustard

1/4 cup rice wine vinegar

Combine rice with water or the broth. Cover, bring to a boil. Simmer for 15 minutes. Remove from heat and leave covered for 10 minutes. Toss, put into bowl to cool. Blanch snow peas 1 minute in lightly salted boiling water. Drain immediately and place in ice water to cool. Drain, pat dry, cut in half on the diagonal. Mix peas, green onion, carrots, pepper, water chestnuts and cilantro into cooled rice. Whisk dressing ingredients until well blended. Toss rice mixture with dressing. Cover and chill until ready to serve. Before serving, sprinkle with almonds. Serves 10-12 generously.

Sally Herrlinger

Teriyaki Chicken & Mango Salad

6 chicken breast halves, boned
and skinned

2 tablespoons peanut oil

1/2 cup Kikkoman teriyaki baste
glaze

6 cups mixed baby greens

1 yellow bell pepper, seeded
and sliced, lengthwise

1 orange bell pepper, seeded
and sliced, lengthwise

2 ripe mangoes, peeled and
sliced, lengthwise

Soy Ginger Vinaigrette:

1/2 cup rice vinegar

1 teaspoon sesame oil

1 teaspoon grated ginger root

1/4 cup peanut or vegetable oil

1 tablespoon soy sauce

Flatten chicken breasts to same thickness. Sauté chicken breasts in skillet with heated peanut oil for 3 minutes on each side. Pour teriyaki baste and glaze over chicken; increase heat, turn chicken repeatedly until glaze covers. Remove chicken and cool. Cut into 1/2 inch strips. Combine greens, peppers and mangoes with chicken. Place ingredients for dressing in a closed container and shake well. Drizzle with Soy Ginger Vinaigrette over all. Serves 6.

Delores Brooks

Tortellini Salad

1 (6 ounce) jar marinated button mushrooms
6 ounces sweet roasted red peppers
1 (14 ounce) can artichoke hearts (non-marinted)
1/4 pound pepperoni, sliced
1/4 pound provolone, sliced
8 ounces tortellini, cooked and cooled
4-5 green onions
Garlic powder
Parmesan cheese
Italian salad dressing

Chop all ingredients into bite size pieces. Mix first 7 ingredients together. Add last 3 ingredients to taste. Refrigerate before serving. Best made 3-4 hours before serving. Serves 8.

Carolyn Sauve

Tropical Pasta Salad

1 (12 ounce) package penne
  pasta, cooked
1 (20 ounce) can pineapple
  chunks
2 cups broccoli florets
1 cup chopped celery
1/2 cup chopped parsley, coarse
1/3 cup chopped green onion
1/3 cup chopped sweet red
  pepper

Dressing:
Salt to taste
Star fruit to garnish
3/4 cup olive oil
1/3 cup balsamic vinegar
2 tablespoons Dijon mustard
2 tablespoons pineapple juice
2 teaspoons dried basil or
  1 tablespoon fresh minced
  basil
1 clove garlic, crushed

You can also use curly pasta...very colorful.

Cook pasta 2 minutes under time suggested on package (do not overcook). Drain and cool. Drain pineapple chunks, reserving 2 tablespoons of juice. Cut chunks in half. Blanch broccoli in boiling water for 30 seconds and cool in ice water. Drain. Chop celery, parsley, green onion and red pepper. For dressing, mix crushed garlic, olive oil, vinegar, mustard, pineapple juice and basil. Add salt to taste. Combine all ingredients and toss together. Chill for a few hours or overnight. Garnish with sliced star fruit. Serves 10-12.

Cherrill Cregar

Tuna Artichoke Salad

2 (6 ounce) cans tuna,
  drained and flaked
1 (16 ounce) jar artichoke
  hearts, drained and chopped

1/4 cup chopped black olives
1/3 cup mayonnaise
1 lemon

Mix tuna with artichoke hearts and olives. Add the mixture of mayonnaise and juice from 1 lemon. Salt and pepper to taste. Serves 4.

Jim Lilliefors

Tuna, Sundried Tomato & Fusilli Pasta Salad

Recipe can be made by substituting equal amounts of canned white albacore tuna.

1 pound Fusilli pasta
7 tablespoons virgin olive oil
4 tuna steaks (5 ounce each
  or 1-inch thick)
4 garlic cloves, finely chopped
3/4 cup thinly sliced, drained,
  oil-packed, sun-dried tomatoes

1/2 cup Italian parsley, chopped
6 tablespoons balsamic vinegar
1/3 cup Kalamata olives, pitted
  and chopped
2 tablespoons drained capers
1 cup fresh chopped basil

Cook pasta until al dente, then drain. Transfer to a large bowl and toss with 2 tablespoons virgin olive oil. Brush tuna with 2 tablespoons olive oil. Sprinkle with salt and pepper. Broil until desired tenderness, about 4 minutes per side, for medium. Cut crosswise into 1/3 inch thick slices. Add to pasta. Heat remaining olive oil (3 tablespoons) and add garlic. Sauté until fragrant, about 1 minute. Stir in tomatoes, then add to pasta and tuna. Add remaining ingredients. Toss. Season with salt and pepper. Serve over a variety of greens. Serves 8.

Sally Lopez

Wild Rice
Seafood Salad

2/3 cup uncooked wild rice
2 cups water
1 teaspoon salt
1/3 cup mayonnaise
1/3 cup sour cream
1/4 cup tomato-based chili
   sauce
1 tablespoon lemon juice
1 teaspoon Dijon-style mustard

1 large tomato, peeled, seeded
   and diced
1 cup thinly sliced celery
1/2 cup thinly sliced green
   onions
1/2 pound crab, shrimp, lobster
   or tuna
Salt and pepper to taste
1 hard boiled egg

Combine wild rice, 2 cups of water and salt in heavy saucepan. Heat until boiling. Reduce heat, cover and simmer 30-45 minutes. Drain and cool. Blend mayonnaise, sour cream, chili sauce, lemon juice and mustard in large bowl. Gently fold in wild rice, tomato, celery, onions and seafood until blended. Season with salt and pepper. Serve in individual lettuce cups. Garnish with parsley and egg slices. Serves 4-6.

Isabelle Hildreth

Wild rice should be cooked for the minimum amount of time required to achieve a tender, attractive product. The grains should be swollen and cracked down the side.

The Art of Cooking • **Soups & Salads**

Vegetables

Artichoke Bake
Artichoke & Spinach Casserole
Asparagus-Artichoke Casserole
Asparagus with Goat Cheese
Au Gratin Cabbage
Aunt Lois' Beans
Blue Cheese Tomatoes
Broccoli Bread
Brussels Sprouts Au Gratin
Buffet Cheese Scalloped Carrots
Carrots Dolce
Cheese Potato Casserole
Corn Soufflé
Eggplant Casserole
Gratin of Four Onions
Greek Green Beans
Holiday Spinach Casserole
Jean's Squash Casserole
Kahlua Sautéed Yams
Marinated Carrots
Mashed Potato Casserole
Meatless Loaf
"Minted Peas" Puree
Onions Celeste
Orange Glazed Asparagus/Mushrooms
Potato Casserole
Roasted Broccoli
Santa Fe Stuffed Peppers
Sauerkraut Casserole
Scalloped Cabbage
Schnitzel Beans
Spinach Casserole
Spinach-Noodle Casserole
String Beans with Tarragon
Sweet Potato Casserole
Tian
Tomato Pie
Zesty Carrot Strips
Zucchini Loaf
Zucchini Tomato Bake

Artichoke Bake

2 cans artichoke hearts
1 small can black olives
1 cup plain bread crumbs

1 teaspoon garlic salt
1/2 cup olive oil

Drain artichokes and slice olives. Mix all ingredients in lightly greased baking dish. Bake for 30 minutes at 350°. Serves 6.

Pat Kumicich

Artichoke & Spinach Casserole

3 (10 ounce) packages frozen chopped spinach (Bird's Eye)

1 (8 ounce) package cream cheese, softened

1 stick butter, softened

1 (6 ounce) can water chestnuts, sliced and chopped

1 (14 ounce) can artichoke hearts, rinsed and drained

Salt and pepper to taste

Buttered bread or cracker crumbs to top

Slightly cook spinach and drain in sieve, squeezing out excess moisture with back of large spoon. Return spinach to pan; add softened butter and cream cheese. Let mixture heat enough to melt and blend, stirring constantly. Add water chestnuts, salt and pepper. Grease or butter a 11/2 or 2-quart baking dish. Rinse artichoke hearts under cold water. Drain and pat dry with a paper towel. Quarter artichokes, removing any tough fibers. Line bottom of baking dish with artichokes. Pour spinach mixture over artichokes. Sprinkle enough buttered bread crumbs or cracker crumbs to cover top of casserole. Heat casserole in 350° oven for 30-45 minutes. May need to lightly cover with foil for the last 5 or 10 minutes to prevent crumbs from burning. Serves 8.

Jo King

Asparagus-Artichoke Casserole

1 can asparagus, pieces or whole, drained	Salt
1 jar marinated artichokes	1 bottle creamy Italian dressing
	1 jar pimientos

Arrange asparagus in shallow casserole serving dish. Slice artichokes in half. Place over asparagus and drizzle oil from jar over both. Shake on a bit of salt. Smother with Italian dressing. Arrange pimiento strips on top. Warm in 300° oven for 20 minutes. Do not overheat. Serves 4.

Gail Webster-Patterson

Asparagus with Goat Cheese

6 slices bacon	31/2-4 ounces goat cheese
2 pounds medium asparagus	2 teaspoons lemon juice
2 tablespoons plus 2 teaspoons olive oil	1 teaspoon lemon rind
	Salt and pepper

Cook and crumble bacon; set aside. Position rack in center of oven and preheat to 500°. Arrange (cleaned and trimmed) asparagus on large rimmed baking sheet. Drizzle with 2 tablespoons of olive oil. Turn to coat well. Sprinkle with salt and pepper. Roast until tender—about 7 minutes. Arrange on platter and sprinkle with crumbled goat cheese, bacon, remaining olive oil, lemon juice and lemon rind. Serves 6.

Jean Beauchamp

You can eliminate the lemon juice in this recipe if you use lemon olive oil.

Au Gratin Cabbage

2 cups shredded cabbage
1/2 cup grated carrots
1/4 cup chopped green onions
1 egg, beaten
1/2 cup milk
3 tablespoons shredded Swiss
   cheese
1/4 teaspoon seasoned salt
1 tablespoon minced fresh
   parsley
1 tablespoon shredded
   Parmesan cheese

In skillet coated with non-stick cooking spray, sauté cabbage, carrots and onions until crisp tender. Transfer to greased, shallow 1-quart baking dish. In a bowl, combine egg, milk, Swiss cheese and salt. Pour over cabbage. Sprinkle with parsley and Parmesan cheese. Bake uncovered at 350° for 30-35 minutes or until knife inserted near the center comes out clean. Serves 2-3.

Dottie Brennan

Aunt Lois' Beans

Bake early the day of serving and reheat for best flavor.

6 (15 ounce) cans butter beans
1 pound bacon, diced
1 cup bean juice
1 cup Karo syrup (dark)
1 cup ketchup
1 cup dark brown sugar
2 tablespoons dry mustard

Drain beans, reserving 1 cup juice. Place in 4-5 quart buttered casserole dish. Combine bean juice, Karo, ketchup, brown sugar and dry mustard in small saucepan. Bring to a boil and simmer for 20 minutes. Distribute bacon and boiled mixture over beans. Bake at 300° for 1 hour. Serves 20.

Jean Barclay

Blue Cheese Tomatoes

12 thick, fresh tomato slices   2/3 cup mayonnaise
2 tablespoons blue cheese

Crumble blue cheese and mash into mayonnaise. Spread mixture on tomato slices. Place on cookie sheet with sides. Broil until mixture bubbles and begins to brown, about 5 minutes. Watch closely. Serves 4-6.

Jane Borchers

Broccoli Bread

4 eggs   1 medium onion
1 stick butter   1 package corn bread mix
1 package chopped broccoli   Salt to taste
1 (6 ounce) container cottage
   cheese

Beat 4 eggs. Melt butter. Steam and drain broccoli. Chop onion. Mix all ingredients together and pour into greased 9"x 9" baking dish. Bake for 25 minutes in a 350° oven or until golden brown. Serves 8-10.

Elizabeth Griffin

Brussels Sprouts
Au Gratin

3 tablespoons butter
1/4 cup flour
Salt and pepper
3/4 cup whole milk
3/4 cup chicken broth

1/2 cup dry white wine
2 pounds fresh brussel
   sprouts, trimmed and cooked
1 cup grated Swiss or Gruyère
   cheese

Make a white sauce with butter, flour, salt and pepper, milk, broth and wine. Gradually stir in cheese and brussel sprouts. Place in chafing dish and serve warm. Serves 6-8.

Anne Steffen

Buffet Cheese
Scalloped Carrots

May make
ahead:
Refrigerate
and bake
uncovered
for 35-45
minutes at
350°.

12 sliced carrots
1/4 cup margarine
1 small onion
1/4 cup flour
1 teaspoon salt
1/4 teaspoon dry mustard

2 cups milk
1/4 teaspoon celery salt
1/8 teaspoon pepper
1/2 pound grated cheddar
   cheese
3 cups buttered bread crumbs

Cook carrots until tender and slice. Sauté onion in margarine for 2-3 minutes. Add flour, salt and dry mustard. Stir in milk until smooth. Add celery salt and pepper. In 2-quart casserole, arrange a layer of carrots; then a layer of cheese. Repeat, ending with carrots. Pour on sauce. Top with crumbs. Bake uncovered for 25 minutes at 350° or until golden. Serves 6-8.

Judy Palay

The Art of Cooking • Vegetables

Carrots Dolce

8 cups carrot slices
1 teaspoon salt
1/2 cup brown sugar

6 tablespoons butter or
  margarine, cubed
1/4 cup chopped fresh mint

Arrange carrots (cut into 1/8-1/4-inch slices) in 3-quart casserole. Sprinkle with salt and sugar. Dot with butter or margarine. Sprinkle fresh mint on top. Bake covered at 350° for 1 hour and 10 minutes. Serves 8.

Anne Ray

Cheese Potato Casserole

8-10 medium to large
  white potatoes
1 pound Velveeta cheese
1 cup mayonnaise

1/2 cup chopped onion
Pepper
1/2 pound bacon, cooked

Boil potatoes in skins, then peel and cube. Mix potatoes, onions and mayonnaise. Cook bacon halfway through. Add 1/2 of bacon to potato mixture. Cut Velveeta into strips. Layer potatoes and Velveeta cheese in 9"x13" pan. Top with remaining bacon (crumbled). Bake at 325° uncovered 45 minutes to 1 hour. Serves 8.

Mary Jane Wall

Corn Soufflé

1 (14 ounce) can whole
  kernel corn
1 (14 ounce) can creamed
  corn
3 eggs

2 tablespoons sugar
2 tablespoons flour
2 heaping tablespoons butter
1/2 cup milk
Salt and pepper

Drain whole kernel corn. In 11/2-quart round soufflé or casserole dish, combine both corns. Beat eggs and add to corn mixture. Add salt and pepper to taste. Mix in sugar, flour and butter. Add milk. Bake at 325° for 11/2 hours. Serves 6-8.

Ann Clayton

Eggplant Casserole

Microwave hard brown sugar for 1 minute.

1 medium eggplant
3/4 teaspoon salt (for boiling
  water)
3 tablespoons butter or
  margarine
3 tablespoons all-purpose flour
1 onion, chopped

1 (28 ounce) can peeled,
  diced tomatoes
1 tablespoon brown sugar
3/4 teaspoon salt
1 cup grated cheddar cheese
1/2 cup dry bread crumbs

Peel and dice eggplant. Cook in salted boiling water for about 10 minutes; then drain. Place in buttered 2-quart casserole dish. Melt butter and stir in flour. Add onions, tomatoes, brown sugar and salt. Cook over low heat, stirring constantly until thick. Pour over eggplant and stir. Combine cheese and bread crumbs. Sprinkle over casserole. Bake at 350° for 30 minutes. Serves 8.

Virginia McNabb

Gratin of Four Onions

1/2 pound shallots, chopped

1 large onion, cut in half and sliced thin

2 bunches leeks (discard tops, slice in half, wash well, slice across thinly)

1 clove garlic, minced

1 bag frozen pearl onions (or fresh onions, cooked until tender)

3 tablespoons butter

2 cups heavy cream or
    2 tablespoons flour and
    2 cups milk

1/4 cup fresh minced parsley

1/2 cup fresh bread crumbs

Grated Parmesan, optional

Sauté the shallots, onion, leeks and garlic in butter very slowly until soft. Add frozen onions and cook just until tender. If using milk, sprinkle 2 tablespoons flour over onions and stir; then add milk. Simmer until cream or milk thickens. Place in buttered baking dish. Sprinkle with bread crumbs, parsley and a few table-spoons of grated Parmesan. Can be made 1-2 days ahead and refrigerated. Bake at 475° for 15-20 minutes until bubbly and crumbs are brown. Serves 8.

Hilda Emerson

Greek Green Beans

2 pounds fresh green beans
2 cups chopped onion
2 garlic cloves, minced
1/2 cup olive oil
2 tablespoons tomato paste

2 large tomatoes, chopped
1/4 cup diced parsley or mint
   (optional)
Salt and pepper to taste
Water

French cut (lengthwise) green beans. Sauté onion and garlic in olive oil until yellow. Add tomato paste and tomatoes. Simmer about 1/2 hour until sauce thickens. Add beans and seasoning and enough water to cover. Cover with lid and cook about 45 minutes until beans are very tender. Sprinkle with parsley or mint if desired. Serves 8.

Beth George

Holiday Spinach Casserole

This is a rich casserole that goes well with bland meats like roast turkey or pork.

4 packages frozen chopped
   spinach
2 (8 ounce) packages cream
   cheese
1/2 pound butter

Salt
Pepper, fresh
1/2 cup bread crumbs
4 tablespoons butter, melted
2 teaspoons sage

Cook spinach in hot water. When done, drain and add cut-up pieces of cream cheese and butter, until blended. Add salt and pepper to taste. Brown bread crumbs in butter; add sage and mix. Pour spinach mixture into greased casserole. Pour bread crumb mixture on top to cover. Cover casserole and bake in 350° oven for 45 minutes. Serves 8.

Arlene Hand

Jean's Squash Casserole

4 medium yellow squash
1 medium onion
1 1/2 cup Pepperidge Farm
  Herb stuffing mix
1 (8 ounce) package shredded
  cheddar cheese

1/2 cup sour cream (can
  substitute with plain yogurt)
1/2-3/4 stick butter or
  margarine

Can be pre-
pared a day
ahead and
refrigerated.
Complements
chicken and
pork roast.

Peel squash and cut into bite-sized chunks. Boil squash in salted water. Drain squash and mash with hand mixer until "mushy." Sauté onion in butter and fold into squash. Fold in sour cream, cheddar cheese (save enough to cover top) and stuffing mix. Bake at 350° for 30-35 minutes until brown and bubbly. Serves 8.

Marty Duncan

Kahlua Sautéed Yams

4 medium-sized yams
1/2 cup butter

1/3 cup brown sugar
1/2 cup Kahlua

Boil yams in large saucepan until tender, but still firm. Cut yams into bite-size pieces. For serving immediately: In a skillet, melt butter with sugar. Add Kahlua and cook 1 minute. Add yams and turn until brown on all sides. Cover and reduce heat and cook for about 15 minutes. Turn yams once more before serving. For preparing ahead of time: Heat butter and sugar in microwave until sugar is dissolved. Add Kahlua to mixture and pour over cooked yams. Completely coat the yams with the sugar/Kahlua mixture and refrigerate overnight or until you are ready to serve. Heat in microwave. Serves 4-6.

Joyce Stack

Marinated Carrots

1 large package raw carrots
2/3 cup oil
1/2 cup sugar
1/2 green pepper, chopped

1/3 cup vinegar
1 cup tomato soup
1 sliced onion

Cook carrots until tender. Slice and cool. Mix all ingredients except carrots to make marinade. Place sliced, cooled carrots in marinade for 24 hours. Serves 6.

Joan Shipman

Mashed Potato Casserole

8 servings instant mashed
  potatoes
1/2-1 cup chopped onion
1 (8 ounce) package cream
  cheese

1 egg
Salt and pepper

Prepare instant mashed potatoes. Stir in onion, cream cheese, egg, salt and pepper. Bake in 350° oven for 1 hour. Serves 6-8.

Louise Leander

Meatless Loaf

1 cup cooked brown rice
2 cups shredded cheddar
  cheese
1 cup wheat germ
1 cup chopped walnuts
1 cup chopped mushrooms
1 large onion, chopped
1/2 cup finely chopped green
  pepper

1/2 cup shredded carrots
5 eggs, lightly beaten
2 tablespoons soy sauce
1 tablespoon prepared
  mustard
1/2 teaspoon thyme

A great sub-
stitute for
meat loaf for
vegetarians.

Combine rice, cheese, wheat germ, nuts, mushrooms, onion, green pepper and carrot. Mix in eggs,
soy sauce, mustard and thyme. Firmly pat into
greased 5"x9" loaf pan. Bake in 350° oven for 55 minutes or until browned. Let stand for 10 minutes. Slice
in pan. Serves 8.

Beech Eastman

"Minted Peas" Puree

3 (10 ounce) packages frozen
  peas, thawed
1/2 cup fresh mint leaves

3 tablespoons milk
3 tablespoons unsalted
  margarine

Cook peas in 3/4 cup of water with mint leaves for
4-5 minutes. Drain. Add milk and margarine. Place in
Cuisinart and pulse; consistency will be like mashed
potatoes. Serves 8.

Sandy Slessinger

Onions Celeste

2 tablespoons butter

2 large sweet onions, sliced and separated in rings

1/2 pound Swiss cheese, grated

1/2 teaspoon salt

1 can cream of chicken soup

1 cup milk

Buttered bread crumbs

Cook onions in butter (steam, do not brown) until tender. Spoon 1/2 onions into a 2-quart casserole and cover with 1/2 grated Swiss cheese. Place 1 layer onions, then 1 layer cheese and repeat. Mix milk with soup and pour over, lifting onions with fork so liquid drains through. Cover with buttered bread crumbs. Bake at 350° for 30 minutes. Serves 6-8.

Nancy Leutheuser

Orange Glazed Asparagus/Mushrooms

1 pound asparagus

1 tablespoon butter

4 ounces fresh slicked shitake mushrooms

1/2 teaspoon salt

Pinch of cayenne

2 teaspoons grated orange

1/3 cup fresh orange juice

Black pepper to taste

Snap off and discard tough ends of asparagus. Cut remaining pieces into thirds. In skillet, melt butter, add asparagus, stir and cook for 4 minutes. Add mushrooms; stir and cook for 3 more minutes. Stir in salt, cayenne, grated orange and orange juice and pepper to taste. Cook covered for 3 minutes more. Transfer to serving platter. Serves 4.

Carol Tweedie

Potato Casserole

2 pounds frozen hash browns
1/4 pound melted butter
1 pint sour cream
1 cup chopped onion
8 ounces sharp cheddar cheese
1 can cream of mushroom soup
2 cups potato chips, crushed

Combine all ingredients except potato chips. Spread in 9"x13" pan or deep casserole. Spread crushed chips on top. Bake in 350° oven for about 1 hour. Serves 8-10.

Ernestine Blum

Roasted Broccoli

2 heads broccoli
2 tablespoons oil
2 tablespoons lemon juice
2 tablespoons sesame oil
2 tablespoons soy sauce
1 teaspoon ground ginger
1 clove garlic, minced
1/4 teaspoon sugar, or to taste
2 teaspoons sesame seeds

Cut 1/2 inch off bottom of broccoli stems. Peel stems with potato peeler to remove tough outer skin. Cut stems diagonally in 1/2 inch slices. Divide tops into serving-size portions. Toss with 2 tablespoons oil. Roast at 500° for 10-12 minutes, until stems can just be pierced with a fork. The broccoli can be microwaved instead of roasting. To microwave, substitute water for oil, and cook on high for 3 minutes. Meanwhile, in blender mix lemon juice, sesame oil, soy sauce, ginger, garlic and sugar. Stir in sesame seeds and pour over hot broccoli. Serve hot or at room temperature. Serves 6.

Sandra Roth

Santa Fe Stuffed Peppers

4 large bell peppers, halved
1 (15 ounce) can corn, drained
1 (15 ounce) can black beans, rinsed

1 cup shredded cheddar cheese
1 cup salsa, medium-hot
1/3 cup chopped cilantro or scallions

Heat broiler and spray broiler pan rack with non-stick cooking spray. Place cored, halved peppers cut side down on rack and broil 7 minutes until lightly charred. In bowl, mix balance of ingredients. Turn peppers over and fill with corn mixture. Broil 2-3 minutes or until filling is hot. Corn mixture can be heated and spooned into peppers before final broiling. Serves 4.

Mary Jo Lombardi

Sauerkraut Casserole

Good with pork!

1 pound bacon, browned
2 tablespoons bacon grease
1 large onion, diced
28 ounces tomatoes, drained

28 ounces sauerkraut, not drained
1 cup brown sugar
1 cup white sugar

Drain bacon reserving 2 tablespoons. Brown or sauté onion in bacon drippings. Add rest of ingredients. Mix and bake at 350° for 1 hour in an 8"x10" glass casserole uncovered. Serves 8-10.

Irma Dralle-Meyer

Scalloped Cabbage

5 cups coarsley shredded
cabbage
2 tablespoons butter
2 tablespoons flour

2 cups milk
1 (4 ounce) package shredded
sharp American cheese
Bread crumbs (buttered)

Cook the cabbage in salted water 10 minutes and drain. Make white sauce with butter, flour and milk. Mix cabbage and white sauce with shredded sharp cheese. Place in 2-quart casserole and refrigerate overnight. Place buttered bread crumbs over casserole. Cook for 45 minutes at 350°. Serves 6-8.

Caroline Drever

Schnitzel Beans

1 1/2 pounds green beans
4 slices bacon, cut up
1 cup sugar

1/2 cup vinegar
1 small onion, chopped

Clean and cut up beans. Cover with water. Simmer for 30 minutes, then drain. Cook bacon until crisp. Add sugar and vinegar. Add beans and onions. Simmer 10 minutes. Serves 4-6.

Kay Wing

Spinach Casserole

3 packages frozen chopped
spinach
1 cup sour cream

1/2 envelope onion soup mix
1/2 cup dry bread crumbs
1 tablespoon butter

Cook and drain spinach. Mix with sour cream and dry onion soup mix. Place in casserole that has been sprayed with Pam. Sprinkle bread crumbs on top and dot with butter. Bake at 350° for 1 hour. Serves 6-8.

Billie Stevens

Spinach-Noodle Casserole

1 package medium-size
noodles
2 packages frozen, chopped
spinach or 2 bunches fresh
spinach

1 can cream of mushroom
soup
1 small jar of Cheese Whiz
Butter or margarine, as desired
1 small can evaporated milk

Cook noodles and spinach separately. Drain. Add soup to spinach. In 2-quart Pyrex dish, put layer of noodles, pads of butter, Cheese Whiz and spinach. Repeat layer. Add salt and pepper to taste. Pour milk over top. Bake at 350° for 1 hour. Serves 8.

Babs Tucker

String Beans with Tarragon

1 pound fresh green beans	1 teaspoon dried tarragon
2 tablespoons unsalted butter	Salt and pepper
2 tablespoons white wine vinegar	Lemon juice to taste
	Freshly grated Parmesan cheese

Cook beans in boiling salted water for approximately 5 minutes. Rinse under cold running water; drain. Mix vinegar and tarragon together and put aside. Melt butter in large skillet over medium heat. Add beans to heat. After beans are warm, add vinegar-tarragon mixture, salt and pepper. Place beans in serving dish and sprinkle with lemon juice. Cover lightly with Parmesan cheese. Serve immediately. Serves 4.

Mickey Baumgartner

Sweet Potato Casserole

1 large can yams, drained and mashed	1/2 teaspoon ground cloves
1 egg	1/4 cup melted butter
1/2 cup brown sugar	Orange juice
1 teaspoon cinnamon	1/4 teaspoon salt
	1 cup whole cranberry sauce

Mix together all ingredients, except cranberry sauce. Use enough orange juice to moisten. Beat with mixer until smooth, adding orange juice if needed. Stir in all but a few teaspoons of whole cranberry sauce. Pour into 2-quart casserole dish or individual ramekins that are buttered. Top with cranberry sauce. Bake at 350° for 30 minutes. Serves 6-8.

Mary Alice French

Tian

This recipe
is French!

1 eggplant, sliced and unpeeled

2 onions, thinly sliced

2 red peppers, seeded and sliced

6 tablespoons olive oil

2 zucchini, sliced thin

3 tablespoons dry bread crumbs

4 garlic cloves, crushed

2 tomatoes, sliced

2 tablespoons Parmesan cheese

Salt, pepper, thyme, rosemary

Sauté eggplant, onions, peppers and garlic in 4 tablespoons olive oil until golden. Spread mixture over bottom of ovenproof dish. Arrange tomatoes and zucchini in alternate rows over top of sautéed vegetable mixture, overlapping them like fish scales. Season with salt, pepper, thyme and rosemary to taste. Cover with bread crumbs. Sprinkle with Parmesan cheese. Bake at 375° for 25 minutes. Serves 6.

Carolyn Sauve

Tomato Pie

5-8 (14 1/2 ounce) cans whole tomoatoes

2 teaspoons baking powder

1/2 teaspoon salt

1 stick margarine

1/2 cup sour cream

1 (8 ounce) package sharp cheddar cheese, shredded

1 cup mayonnaise

1 cup chopped onions

Drop of baking powder

Seasoned pepper to taste

Shortcut: Diced tomaotes and pre-made pie shell can be substituted.

Tomatoes must be drained for 2 days prior to making the pie. Press to squeeze out liquid and pull apart tomatoes to make small pieces. When ready to make pie—mix the flour, baking powder and salt. Cut in margarine and then add sour cream. Roll out and place in greased 9" or 10" pie plate. Place drained tomatoes in mixing bowl and add next 5 ingredients. Place tomatoe mixture into pie shell and bake at 375° for 35-45 minutes. Serves 8.

Joyce Yamron

Zesty Carrot Strips

6 pounds carrots

4 teaspoons minced onion

4 tablespoons horseradish

1 cup mayonnaise

1 teaspoon salt

1/2 teaspoon ground black pepper

Paprika

Buttered bread crumbs

Boil carrots after cleaning and cutting into strips. Test with fork to ensure tenderness. In small mixing bowl, mix dried minced onion, horseradish, mayonnaise, salt and pepper. Layer carrots and horseradish mixture in oven-safe baking dish, top with bread crumbs and sprinkle with paprika. (This much can be done ahead of time.) Bake at 350° for 15 minutes. Serves 8.

Sally Mauger Veil

Zucchini Loaf

1 cup Bisquick

4 eggs

4 ounces grated Parmesan cheese

1/2 cup vegetable oil

3 medium zucchini, coarsely grated

1 medium onion, finely chopped

1 clove garlic, finely chopped

Mix all ingredients. Place in greased 10"x6" loaf pan and bake at 350° for 40-45 minutes. Serves 4-6.

Sally Blumenfeld

Zucchini Tomato Bake

1/4 cup salad oil
1 small clove of garlic
6 small unpeeled zucchini, sliced
1 1/2 teaspoons seasoned salt
1/2 cup shredded sharp cheese
1/4 cup grated Parmesan cheese

4 medium tomatoes, peeled and sliced
1/2 cup dry bread crumbs
2 tablespoons butter or margarine, melted

Heat oil in skillet. Cook garlic for 2-3 minutes. Remove and discard. Sauté zucchini in oil until lightly browned. Combine seasoned salt and cheeses. Make alternate layers in casserole of zucchini and tomatoes. Sprinkle each layer with cheeses. Toss crumbs and butter and spread on top. Bake at 350° for 25 minutes. Serves 6.

Carol Conant

notes and recipes

The Art of Cooking • **Vegetables**

Brunch

Anne's Southern Breakfast Casserole
Baked Eggs in Brioche
Baked French Toast
Brandied Fruit
Breakfast Break
Corn Fritters
Curried Apples
Dilly Casserole Bread
Egg-Mushroom-Sausage Soufflé
Garlic Cheese Grits Casserole
Hot Corn Cakes
Huevos Rancheros
Lemon Cottage Cheese Pancakes
Oven Puffed French Toast
Overnight Ham & Cheese Bake
Pineapple Soufflé
Soufflé Sandwich with Crabmeat
Sour Cream Coffee Cake
Stuffed French Bread
Sweet Noodle Kugel Pudding

Breads

Bran Muffins
Cheese Bread
Cranberry-Orange Scones
Easy Banana Bread
Easy Cinnamon Buns
Gina's 1-Hour Heavy Bread
Kentucky Spoon Bread
Rag Muffins
Vermont Maple Muffins
Wheat Germ Coffee Cake
Zucchini Bread

Anne's Southern Breakfast Casserole

8 cups water

2 cups grits (not instant)

2 pounds bulk sausage, browned

2 cups sharp cheddar, grated

3 tablespoons butter

3 eggs, beaten

3 or 4 dashes Tabasco

3 cloves garlic, pressed

1/3 cup fresh parsley, chopped

Prepare grits according to package directions. Add all other ingredients and bake in buttered round 4-quart baking dish or dutch oven for 45 minutes at 350°. Serve with a side of fresh fruit. Serves 10-12.

Anne Steffen

I use hot sausage mixed with sage sausage, half and half. You could also use kielbasa.

Baked Eggs in Brioche

4 small brioche

2 tablespoons unsalted
butter

4 large eggs

1 tablespoon chopped fresh
chives

Salt

Pepper

Preheat oven to 350°. Cut off top of brioche (about 1 inch not counting knob). Scoop out insides to make a shell, leaving about 1/4"-1/3" all around. Don't tear the shell. Melt the butter and brush the inside and outside of top with melted butter. Arrange brioche in a muffin tin. Crack an egg into each brioche; salt and pepper, to taste. Bake brioche in lower third of oven for 15 minutes. Arrange brioche tops on cookie sheet. Put in upper third of oven. Bake bottoms and tops until eggs are done, about 8-10 minutes. Watch closely for desired egg consistency as oven temperatures may vary. Remove from oven and sprinkle chives over eggs. Serve each brioche with its top. Serves 4.

Herbert Rowe

Baked French Toast

1 cup brown sugar

1/2 cup butter

2 tablespoons corn syrup

1 loaf French bread, cut into
3/4-inch slices

5 eggs

1 1/2 cups milk

1 teaspoon vanilla

Powdered sugar

In a saucepan over medium low heat, mix and melt brown sugar, butter and syrup. Spray a 9"x13" pan with non-stick vegetable oil and pour butter/sugar/syrup mixture into it. Arrange bread slices on top of the mixture in a pan. In a blender mix eggs, milk and vanilla. Pour egg mixture over bread slices, using all of mixture. Cover and refrigerate overnight. Next day, preheat oven to 350°. Uncover pan and bake for 30 minutes or until toast is light golden brown. Sprinkle toast with powdered sugar and serve immediately. Serves 8.

Sylvia Ketterman

Brandied Fruit

2 cups sugar

2 cups water

2 inch stick cinnamon

1 can peach halves

1 can pear halves

1 can apricot halves

1 1/2 cups liquid from canned
fruit

1 1/2 cups fruit flavored brandy

1/4 cup whole cloves

1/4 cup whole allspice

Drain fruit, reserving 1 1/2 cups liquid. Boil together the sugar, water, liquid from the can, and cinnamon until thickened. Add the brandy. Place fruit in large glass container. Add cloves and allspice. Pour liquid mixture over fruit. Chill overnight. Serves 8.

Helen Stephens

Breakfast Break

6 slices buttered bread

6 eggs

2 cups milk

1 teaspoon salt

1/2 teaspoon dry mustard

1 pound sausage or bacon

1/2 cup cheddar cheese, shredded

Grease 13"x9" pan with butter. Place 6 buttered slices of bread on bottom of pan. Beat 6 eggs, milk, salt and mustard. Brown sausage or bacon. Crumble and sprinkle on top of bread. Pour liquid mixture on top and sprinkle with cheese. Cover and refrigerate overnight. Bake for 45 minutes at 350°. Serves 6.

Katherine Wielgus

Corn Fritters

2 cups corn (cut from cooked corn on the cob)

1/2 cup milk

2 eggs, beaten

1 cup flour

2 teaspoons baking powder

1/2 teaspoon salt

Dash of pepper

Add milk to corn; add eggs to dry ingredients. Combine. Drop batter by tablespoons full into 2" of hot cooking oil. Fry until golden brown. Serve immediately with real maple syrup. Serves 4-6.

Joyce Vitelli

Curried Apples

4 medium firm apples
  (Winesap or Granny Smith)
3 tablespoons butter

2 tablespoons brown sugar
2 teaspoons curry powder
1/8 teaspoon salt

Core but do not peel apples. Slice 1/4-1/2" thick to make rings. Mix butter, brown sugar, curry powder and salt. Place a little water (3-4 tablespoons) in bottom of a 9"x13" baking dish. Spread apples with curry mixture and arrange in baking dish. Broil until lightly browned. Serves 4.

Jane Borchers

Dilly Casserole Bread

1 package yeast
1/4 cup warm water
1 cup creamed cottage cheese
2 tablespoons sugar
1 tablespoon instant onion
1 tablespoon butter or
  margarine

2 teaspoons dill seed
1 teaspoon salt
1/8 teaspoon soda
1 unbeaten egg
21/4-21/2 cups flour

Soften yeast in water. Combine all ingredients, except flour, which you add gradually, beating well after each addition to form stiff dough. Cover. Let rise until double in size (about 1 hour). Stir down. Turn into well-greased 8-inch round casserole. Let rise again in warm place (30-40) minutes. Then bake 40-50 minutes at 350° until golden brown. Brush with soft butter and sprinkle with salt. Good cold if any is left. Serves 6-8.

Pat DeReamer-Surgener

Egg-Mushroom-Sausage Soufflé

8 slices of bread (remove crusts)

2 cups sharp cheddar cheese, grated

1 pound link sausage, browned and cut into 1-inch cubes

8 eggs, beaten

1/8 teaspoon salt

2 1/2 cups milk

3/4 teaspoon dry mustard

Pinch of Beau Monde seasoning

1 can mushroom soup

1/2 can milk

Cayenne pepper, to taste

Garlic salt, to taste

Fresh mushrooms (optional)

Cube bread slices and place half in bottom of 3-quart casserole. Sprinkle half of the grated cheese; then half of the sausage cubes (cut into 1-inch cubes). Repeat this process until all ingredients are in the dish. Mix eggs, salt, milk, mustard and Beau Monde seasoning. Pour over bread. Mix 1 can of mushroom soup with 1/2 can milk. Spread on top of mixture. Season with cayenne pepper and garlic salt. Top with sliced fresh mushrooms. Bake 1 1/2 hours at 300°. Serves 8-9.

Jean Sampson

Garlic Cheese Grits Casserole

1 cup grits
1 roll garlic cheese
1 stick oleo

2 eggs, beaten
Milk

Cook 1 cup grits following directions on box. Remove from heat. Stir in 1 roll of garlic cheese, 1 stick of oleo and 2 eggs beaten, which have been put into measuring cup and milk added to measure 1 cup. Pour into greased 2-quart casserole and bake in 400° oven for 30-45 minutes. Serves 10-12.

Janet Flowers

Hot Corn Cakes

1 egg, beaten
1 tablespoon sugar
1/2 teaspoon salt
2 tablespoons melted butter

1 cup buttermilk
1 teaspoon baking soda
2 tablespoons flour
1 cup yellow cornmeal

Mix beaten egg, sugar, salt and butter. Combine buttermilk and soda and stir in. Add flour and cornmeal. Stir only until moist (batter may be slightly lumpy). Pour onto hot griddle. Turn cakes as soon as they are puffed and full of bubbles. Serve with butter and maple syrup immediately. Serves 2-3.

Marjorie White

Huevos Rancheros

Great with fresh fruit platter, toasted tortillas and ham, sausage or bacon.

3 tablespoons oil
1 onion
1 green pepper
4 cloves garlic
11/2 teaspoons salt/pinch pepper
1 tablespoon flour
11/2 teaspoons chili powder
1 teaspoon cumin
2 large cans tomatoes, diced and drained
1 teaspoon sugar
10-14 eggs
2 cups Monterey Jack cheese, shredded

Dice onion and green pepper. Place in large skillet with oil, garlic, salt and pepper. Simmer until soft. Stir in flour, chili powder and cumin. Add tomatoes and sugar. Simmer and put aside or freeze until needed. (Tomato mixture freezes well.) On the day of serving, scramble 10-14 eggs. Spray 9"x13" casserole with oil. Put eggs in casserole. Cover eggs with tomato mixture. Place shredded cheese on top. Bake at 350° for 30 minutes. Serves 8.

Kay Bendheim

Lemon Cottage Cheese Pancakes

3 eggs, separated
1/4 cup flour
3/4 cup cottage cheese
1/4 cup unsalted butter, melted
2 tablespoons sugar
1/4 teaspoon salt
1-2 teaspoon grated lemon zest

Raspberry Sauce:
1 (10 ounce) package frozen
  raspberries, thawed
1/2 cup sugar
2 tablespoons lemon juice

Separate eggs and beat egg whites until they hold soft peaks. In another bowl, stir together rest of ingredients. Fold egg whites into yolk mixture and gently stir. Ladle spoonful of batter into skillet at medium heat (325°-350°) for about 11/2 minutes and turn. (Use unsalted butter on skillet.) Dust with powdered sugar and garnish with a strawberry. Serve with raspberry sauce or maple syrup. For the raspberry sauce, combine raspberries and sugar. Cook 20-25 minutes. Add lemon juice last and cook for a few minutes. Strain and cool. Makes 12-16 pancakes

Diane Lupean

Oven Puffed French Toast

8 slices French bread, cut 1 1/2 inches thick

6 eggs

1/8 teaspoon nutmeg

1/4 teaspoon cinnamon

1 teaspoon vanilla

3 cups Half and Half

Topping:

1/2 cup firm butter, cubed

1 cup brown sugar

1 cup nuts, pieces

Place bread slices in a single layer in a generously buttered 9"x13"x 2" baking pan. Combine eggs, spices, vanilla and Half and Half, mixing well. Pour over bread slices; cover and refrigerate overnight. Before baking, baste unabsorbed liquid over bread. Combine topping ingredients until mixture resembles a coarse texture. Sprinkle over bread slices and bake in preheated oven at 350° for 40 minutes. Serves 8.

Helene Gradolph

Overnight Ham & Cheese Bake

8 slices bread

2 tablespoons butter

2 cups grated cheddar cheese

3/4 pound diced ham

1/2 pound mushrooms

7 ounces diced chiles

2 cups Monterey Jack cheese

6 eggs

2 cups milk

1/2 teaspoon dry mustard

1/4 teaspoon onion salt

1/2 teaspoon salt, paprika and pepper

Remove crust from bread and butter. Place bread butter-side down in 9"x13" baking dish. Sprinkle with cheddar cheese. Sauté and layer sliced ham, mushrooms and chiles on top of bread. Sprinkle with grated Monterey Jack cheese. Beat eggs and milk with seasonings. Pour over ingredients and refrigerate overnight. Bake in preheated oven at 325° for 50 minutes. Remove from oven and let stand for 10 minutes to set before serving. Serves 8-10.

Ona Nelson

Pineapple Soufflé

3 eggs
11/4 cups sugar
2 tablespoons flour
1 large can crushed pineapple

1/2 pound butter or 2 sticks
margarine
6 slices Pepperidge Farms
white bread, cubed

Beat together eggs, sugar and flour. Add thoroughly drained pineapple and set aside. In fry pan, melt butter and toss bread cubes until golden. Blend with other ingredients and pour into baking dish, approximately 11/2 to 2-quart size. Bake at 350° for 45 minutes. Serves 8.

Fran Gilbert

Soufflé Sandwich with Crabmeat

16 slices buttered bread, crust removed
8 slices Swiss cheese
1 large can crabmeat, shredded
5 eggs

3 cups milk
2 teaspoon salt
Parmesan cheese
Watercress or parsley for garnish

Butter a large, shallow rectangular baking dish. Place half the bread slices into pan, buttered-side down. Lay cheese slices on bread. Sprinkle crabmeat on cheese. Beat together eggs, milk and salt in bowl. Place remaining 8 slices of bread on top of crabmeat. Pour egg mixture over all. Top with Parmesan cheese generously. Refrigerate overnight for at least 8 hours. Bake 1 hour at 325°. Serves 8.

Dottie Brennan

Sour Cream Coffee Cake

1 cup sugar
1/2 pound margarine
2 eggs, beaten
1 teaspoon vanilla
1/4 teaspoon salt
2 cups unsifted flour
1 teaspoon baking powder

1 teaspoon baking soda
1/2 pint sour cream

Topping:
1/2 cup brown sugar
1/2 cup nuts
2 teaspoons cinnamon

Cream margarine and sugar. Beat eggs and add vanilla, salt, flour, baking powder, baking soda and sour cream. Mix topping of brown sugar, nuts and cinnamon together. In a well-greased bundt pan 10"x4", put 1/2 batter and then 1/2 topping. Repeat. Bake for 55 minutes at 375°. After cooking turn upside down on platter. Serves 10.

Sally Roberts

Stuffed French Bread

1 loaf French bread
8 ounces cream cheese
12 eggs

2 cups milk
1/3 cup maple syrup
Cinnamon sugar

Cube the bread and cream cheese. Layer 1/2 the bread with 1/2 the cream cheese. Add second layer with 1/2 bread and 1/2 cream cheese. Beat eggs, milk and syrup together. Pour over bread and cream cheese. Refrigerate overnight. Bake at 350° for 35-30 minutes, until knife comes out clean. Serve sprinkled with cinnamon sugar and warm syrup. Serves 8.

Mary Jane Wall

Sweet Noodle Kugel Pudding

Brown sugar
1 pound broad noodles
1/2 pound butter
4 eggs
4-5 fresh apples or peaches, peeled and sliced

3/4 cup white raisins
1 (8 ounce) jar apricot preserves
2-3 tablespoons cinnamon-sugar mixture

Grease bottom of pan with butter and sprinkle with brown sugar for a glazing effect when kugel is turned out. Cook noodles; drain and mix with other ingredients. Bake at 350° in 9"x13" pan for 11/2 hours. Cover with aluminum foil if it gets too brown. Serves 12+.

Pauline Hendel

Bran Muffins

1 cup water
1 cup 100% Bran (Nabisco)
11/4 cup sugar
1/2 cup butter or margarine
2 eggs
21/2 cups flour

21/2 teaspoons baking soda
2 cups Kellogg's All Bran
2 cups buttermilk
11/2 cups white or brown
  raisins

Pour 1 cup boiling water over 100% Bran; then cool. Cream sugar, butter or margarine and eggs. Add soaked Bran. Mix together flour, soda and All Bran. Then add buttermilk and raisins. Bake at 350° in tins for 15-20 minutes. Batter can be kept in a sealed container in the refrigerator for up to 2-3 weeks. Makes 2-3 dozen muffins.

Jean Barclay

Cheese Bread

1 cup water
1/4 pound butter
1 teaspoon salt
3 dashes of pepper

1 cup flour
4 eggs
1 cup sharp cheddar cheese,
  shredded

Combine water, butter, salt and pepper in a saucepan. Bring to a boil. Add flour and cook and stir until mixture forms a ball. Remove from heat. Beat in eggs, 1 at a time. Stir in cheese. Grease baking sheet. Preheat oven to 425°. Drop dough on cookie sheet, making a ring. Bake for 45 minutes. Serves 8-10.

Kay Wing

Cranberry-Orange Scones

1/2 cup butter, melted	1 tablespoon baking powder
1/3 cup milk	1/4 teaspoon salt
1 large egg	1 teaspoon cream of tartar
11/2 cups flour	1/2 cup dried cranberries
11/4 cups Quick Quaker Oats	1/3 cup grated orange rind
1/4 cup sugar	

Mix butter, milk and egg in a small bowl. Put dry ingredients in a large bowl (flour, oats, sugar, baking powder, salt and cream of tartar). Add the wet ingredients to the dry ingredients in a large bowl. Mix together until dry ingredients are moistened. Last, add the cranberries and grated orange rind. Shape dough to form 2 balls. Pat out on a floured surface to form two 8-inch circles. Cut each circle into 6 wedges, making 12 scones. Bake on greased cookie sheet in hot oven at 425° for 15 minutes or until golden brown. Serve with butter, honey, or lemon rind. Makes 12 scones.

Barbara Hennig

Easy Banana Bread

1/2 cup salad oil	2 cups mashed bananas,
2 cups sugar	(5 bananas)
4 eggs	41/2 cups Bisquick

Preheat oven to 350°. Cream oil and sugar. Add eggs and beat on "stir." Mix in mashed bananas and add Bisquick. Bake in 3 greased loaf pans for about 45 minutes or until toothpick inserted is clean. Makes 3 loaves.

Anne Lynn

Easy Cinnamon Buns

Nuts

Raisins

24 Rich's frozen dinner rolls

1 package butterscotch pudding

1/2 cup melted butter

1/2 cup brown sugar

1 teaspoon cinnamon

Grease and flour 10"x15" pan. Sprinkle nuts and raisins in bottom of pan. Arrange rolls in pan and sprinkle with pudding mix (not instant). Combine melted butter and brown sugar and pour over rolls. Sprinkle with cinnamon. Cover with foil and let rise in unheated oven overnight. Remove foil and bake at 350° for 25 minutes. Turn out of pan immediately. Makes 24 rolls.

Marjorie White

Must use regular pudding mix— not instant. Turn out of pan immediately after baking.

Gina's 1-Hour Heavy Bread

3 cups flour

1/2 cup dry milk

1 1/2 teaspoons salt

2 packages yeast

1/4 cup sugar

2 cups All Bran

1 1/2 cup warm water

1 egg

1/3 cup margarine or butter

Mix dry ingredients: flour, dry milk and salt. Set aside. Mix yeast, sugar, water and All Bran. Let stand 2 minutes. Add egg and margarine or butter. Mix 1 cup of dry ingredient mixture that you have set aside and beat into egg/butter mix on low speed for 2 minutes. Add rest of dry ingredient mixture. Cover and let rise until double in size. Punch down and place in greased loaf pan. Bake at 375° for 40 minutes. Makes 1 loaf.

Laura Woodhams

You may add 1 tablespoon molasses.

Kentucky Spoon Bread

1/2 cup corn meal, white or
yellow

2 cups milk

3 tablespoons butter

1/2 teaspoon salt

3 eggs, well beaten

Mix corn meal and milk in saucepan. Bring to a boil. Remove from heat and add butter and salt. Let cool about 30 minutes. Beat eggs for 3 minutes. Fold beaten eggs into cornmeal mixture. Pour into 2-quart buttered casserole. Bake in preheated 350°oven for 45 minutes or until knife blade comes out clean. Serves 4.

Elizabeth Perkins

Rag Muffins

2 cups enriched flour

2 teaspoons baking powder

1/4 teaspoon salt

1 tablespoon shortening

3/4 cup milk

4 teaspoons soft butter or
margarine

5 tablespoons sugar

Sift flour, measure, sift again with baking powder and salt into small mixing bowl. Cut shortening into flour. Add milk and mix well. Knead about 30 seconds on lightly floured board. Roll out into rectangle (9"x15"). Spread with softened butter and sprinkle with sugar. Roll up like a jelly roll. Seal edge and cut into 1-inch slices. Place cut side down in well-greased muffin pans. Bake at 400° for 20 minutes or until browned. Makes 12 muffins.

Cynthia Quick

Vermont Maple Muffins

13/4 cups flour
1/4 teaspoon baking powder
1 teaspoon baking soda
1 cup sugar
3 teaspoons cinnamon
1/2 teaspoon salt
1/2 cup wheat bran

1/2 cup pecans, chopped
2 eggs
1/2 cup oil
1 cup canned pumpkin
1/4 cup water
4 tablespoons maple syrup
1/3 cup carrots, grated

Mix together dry ingredients and pecans. In another bowl, beat together eggs, oil, pumpkin, water, maple syrup and carrots. Add wet ingredients to dry ingredients, mixing just until combined. Spoon into greased muffin tins, 3/4 full. Bake at 375° for 25-30 minutes. Makes 12 muffins.

Jini Horan

Wheat Germ Coffee Cake

1/2 cup wheat germ
1/2 cup sugar
1 cup brown sugar
1/2 cup vegetable oil
1 teaspoon cinnamon

1 cup buttermilk
1 teaspoon baking soda
11/2 cups flour, unbleached
1/4 teaspoon salt
1/2 cup nuts

Mix wheat germ, sugar, brown sugar, oil and cinnamon. Reserve 1 cup of above mixture. Add together buttermilk, soda, flour and salt. Combine and mix well with reserved 1 cup topping. Pour into 9"x12" (or smaller) pan. Top with remaining wheat germ mixture and nuts. Bake at 350° for 30 minutes. Serves 8.

Mary Ann Bindley

Zucchini Bread

3 eggs

2 cups granulated sugar

1 cup vegetable oil

2 cups grated, peeled raw
zucchini

3 teaspoons vanilla extract

2 cups all-purpose flour

1 teaspoon salt

1 teaspoon baking soda

1/2 teaspoon baking powder

3 teaspoons cinnamon

1 cup walnuts

Beat eggs until light and foamy. Add sugar, oil, zucchini and vanilla. Mix lightly, but well. Combine flour, salt, baking soda, baking powder and cinnamon. Add to egg/zucchini mixture. Stir until well blended and add nuts. Pour into (2) greased 9"x5"x3" loaf pans. Bake in preheated 350° oven for 1 hour. Cool on rack. Makes 2 loaves.

Joe & Barrie Batchelder

Pasta

Artichoke Pasta Sauce
Asparagus Pasta Stir Fry
Cherry Creek Orzo
Chicken & Broccoli Pasta
Lasagna
Linguine with Meat Sauce
Linguine with Tomatoes & Basil
Marco Italian Spaghetti Sauce
Pasta alla Peperonata
Pasta Carbonara
Pasta with Sausage & Chicken
Penne all Arrabbiata
Penne alla Maria
Penne alla Vodka
Penne with Broccoli Rabe
Penne Pasta Marinara
Pink & Green Shrimp & Green Noodles
Pizzaghetti
Puttanesca Sauce
Ravioli with Walnut Sauce
Salmon Salad Shells
Spaghetti Giovanni
Spaghetti Pie
Special Spaghetti Sauce
Spinach Lasagna
Tortellini per Tutti
Veal Osso Buco over Pasta

Rice

Armenian Rice
Curried Rice
Gilda's Rice
Green Chili/Cheese Rice Casserole
Hawaiian Fried Rice
Rice Chantilly
Rice & Noodle Casserole
Risotto with Mushrooms & Pea Pods
Saffron Rice
Swedish Rice
Wild Rice

Artichoke Pasta Sauce

2 (6 ounce) jars marinated
artichoke hearts

1 tablespoon butter or corn oil

1 cup sliced onions

2 teaspoons dried basil

1/2 cup sour cream

1/2 cup cottage cheese

Cayenne, salt, pepper

Parmesan to sprinkle

Cooked pasta for 4
(raddiatore or penne)

Drain artichoke liquid into skillet. Chop artichoke hearts into bite-size pieces and reserve. Add butter to liquid, heat to medium-high, add onions and sauté until soft. Add artichoke hearts and basil. Cook for 5 minutes. Reduce heat and add sour cream, cheese, cayenne pepper, salt and pepper and stir until heated through. Don't boil. Toss with pasta and sprinkle with Parmesan. Serves 4.

Lynda Bulloch

Asparagus Pasta Stir Fry

1 pound fresh asparagus

1/2 cup sliced onion

2 tablespoons olive oil

2 tablespoons soy sauce

1 clove minced garlic

1 teaspoon grated ginger root

1/2 teaspoon Worcestershire
sauce

1/8 teaspoon crushed red
pepper

6 ounces angel hair pasta,
cooked

You may also add shrimp or chicken.

Slice asparagus into 2-inch pieces. Stir-fry asparagus and onion in oil until tender. Add seasonings and mix well. Add cooked pasta and stir-fry until thoroughly heated and evenly mixed. Serves 6.

Judy Driscoll

Cherry Creek Orzo

6 cups water
1/2 teaspoon saffron
1 cup uncooked orzo pasta
2/3-1 cup dried cranberries or cherries
3-4 green onions, sliced
3 tablespoons slivered toasted almonds

Dressing:
2 tablespoons fresh orange juice
3 tablespoons olive oil
4 teaspoons orange zest
Salt to taste

Bring 6 cups of water to a boil. Add saffron. Add orzo and cook until al dente (8 minutes). Drain and set aside. In a small bowl combine zest and orange juice. Slowly whisk in oil. Add salt and combine orzo, cherries, almonds and onions. Toss with dressing. Serve at room temperature. Serves 4-6.

Carolyn Davis

Chicken & Broccoli Pasta

1/4 cup extra virgin olive oil

2 garlic cloves, finely chopped

1/2 pound boneless, skinless chicken breasts

11/4 cups small broccoli flowerets

3/4 cup oil-packed sun-dried tomatoes, drained and thinly sliced

1 teaspoon dried basil leaves

1 pinch crushed red pepper flakes

Salt and pepper to taste

1/4 cup dry white wine

3/4 cup chicken broth

1 tablespoon butter

1/2 pound bowtie pasta (cooked according to package)

Heat oil over medium heat in a large skillet. Sauté garlic about 1 minute until golden, stirring constantly. Cut chicken into 1/2-inch wide strips and sauté until white—almost completely cooked. Add broccoli and sauté until crisp-tender; add sun-dried tomatoes, basil leaves, red pepper flakes, salt and pepper. Stir in wine, broth and butter. Cook for 3-5 minutes or until heated through, stirring occasionally. Toss freshly cooked pasta with chicken mixture. Serves 4.

Lori Sherman

Lasagna

Use no-boil lasagna strips—it works! Use foil throwaway pan for easy cleanup and make ahead and freeze, if desired.

2 large cans chopped tomatoes
2 cans tomato soup
1 tablespoon oregano
3 garlic cloves, diced
1/4 cup grated Parmesan cheese
Salt and pepper to taste
1 large chopped onion
1/2 pound ground pork
11/2 pounds ground beef
1 box no-boil lasagna
1 pint ricotta (mixed with an egg)
1 (16 ounce) package whole mozzarella cheese
1/2 pound sliced American cheese

Combine first 6 ingredients and begin to simmer. Brown onion, pork and beef. Add to sauce. Simmer for 2 hours. Spray or grease deep foil pan. Add 3 lasagna strips, spread ricotta, top with sauce; then add 3 lasagna strips, sliced mozzarella, top with sauce and add 3 more lasagna strips, American cheese and top with sauce. Sprinkle top layer with Parmesan. Bake at 350° for 30-40 minutes. Serves 8-10.

Naomi Morris

Linguine with Meat Sauce

2 pounds ground beef
1 (28 ounce) can crushed
tomatoes
1 (8 ounce) can tomato sauce
1 (6 ounce) can tomato paste
1 teaspoon salt
2 teaspoons sugar

8 ounces linguine, uncooked
1 (16 ounce) sour cream
1 (8 ounce) cream cheese,
softened
1 bunch green onions, chopped
2 cups sharp cheddar cheese,
shredded

Cook beef in Dutch oven, stirring until beef crumbles. Stir in tomatoes and next 4 ingredients. Simmer for 30 minutes; set aside. Cook pasta according to package directions, then drain. Place pasta in a lightly greased 13"x9" dish. Stir together sour cream, cream cheese and green onions. Spread over pasta. Top with meat sauce. Bake at 350° for 20-25 minutes. Sprinkle with cheddar cheese and bake 5 minutes or until cheese melts. Let stand 5 minutes. Serves 8.

Marilyn Perry

Linguine with Tomatoes & Basil

May substitute cooked shrimp for Brie, but do not marinate the shrimp.

4 large ripe tomatoes, cut in 1/2 inch pieces

1 pound Brie cheese, rind removed (cut in cubes)

1 cup cleaned, fresh basil, cut in strips

3 garlic cloves, finely diced

1 cup plus 1 tablespoon olive oil

21/2 teaspoons salt

1/2 teaspoon freshly ground pepper

11/2 pound linguine

Freshly grated Parmesan cheese

Into large bowl, place tomatoes, Brie, basil, chopped garlic, 1 cup olive oil, 1/2 teaspoon salt and pepper. Cover and leave at room temperature at least 2 hours. Bring 6 quarts water (with 1 tablespoon olive oil and 2 teaspoons salt) to a boil in a large pot. Add linguine and boil until tender, about 8-10 minutes, drain pasta and immediately toss with tomato sauce. Serve at once with salad and crusty bread. Serves 4-6.

Elsie Schneider

Marco Italian Spaghetti Sauce

1 1/2 pounds round steak, ground

1 medium-sized onion, finely chopped

3 tablespoons olive oil

1 clove garlic

2 large cans Italian tomatoes

1 small can Italian tomato paste

1 tablespoon salt

1 teaspoon sugar

1/2 teaspoon red pepper seed

3 pinches of finely chopped parsley

2 tablespoons grated Parmesan cheese

Brown meat and onion in a frying pan; drain off liquid. Brown garlic and olive oil together in a large pot. Press tomatoes through strainer and add to pot. Bring to a slow boil. Add paste, salt, sugar, pepper seeds and blend in. Simmer and stir occasionally for 2 hours. Add parsley, cheese and meat. Simmer for 1/2 hour. Serve over favorite pasta. Serves 6.

Ellen & Vince Kiernan

Pasta alla Peperonata

Can prepare
sauce ahead.
Less pasta
makes the
delicious
sauce more
dominant.

1/4 cup olive oil
1 medium-sized red onion,
   thinly sliced
2 cloves garlic, chopped
6 red and yellow sweet
   peppers, sliced in strips
3 tablespoons balsamic vinegar
1 (14 ounce) can plum
   tomatoes and juice or 1 can
   chopped tomatoes and juice

3/4-1 pound uncooked penne
   pasta
Grated Parmesan cheese
1/4 cup chopped fresh flat
   leaf parsley
Salt and pepper to taste

Sauté onion and garlic in oil in large 12-inch frying pan, 5 minutes until onion softens. Add peppers and cook for 2-3 minutes; add vinegar. Reduce heat to medium and cover, stirring occasionally for about 30 minutes. When peppers are tender, add tomatoes and cook 15 minutes longer. Salt and pepper to taste. Cook pasta in boiling water, 7-10 minutes until tender, but firm. Combine pasta and sweet pepper sauce in serving bowl. Add cheese and parsley. Serve hot. Serves 6.

Joyce Kelly

Pasta Carbonara

1 pound cooked, diced bacon
2 teaspoons salt
1 pound spaghetti or linguine
3 eggs

1/3 cup chopped parsley
Fresh grated Parmesan cheese
Fresh ground black pepper to
taste

Cook pasta in salted boiling water al dente (not mushy). Meanwhile, beat eggs in large serving bowl. Drain pasta. Pour immediately into bowl of eggs and toss. (Heat from pasta cooks the eggs.) Sprinkle bacon and parsley over pasta and toss. Top with Parmesan and pepper. Serves 4-6.

Patricia Dirks

Pasta with
Sausage & Chicken

3 tablespoons olive oil

2 skinless chicken breasts, halved and cut into 1-inch pieces

1/2 cup dry white wine

1 pound mild Italian sausage, casings removed

2 cups chopped onions

1 (14 1/2 ounce) can diced tomatoes in juice

1 1/4 cup low-salt chicken broth

2 tablespoons tomato paste

1 tablespoon minced garlic

12 ounces farfalle pasta

1 1/2 cups freshly grated Parmesan cheese

1/4 cup chopped Italian parsley

Sauté chicken in hot oil for about 5 minutes. Transfer chicken to a bowl. Add wine to skillet; boil until reduced to 2 tablespoons, scraping up browned bits, about 3 minutes. Pour wine over chicken. Add onions and sausage to same skillet and cook until sausage browns; breaking up with back of spoon, about 10 minutes. Mix in tomatoes with juice, broth, tomato paste and garlic. Simmer about 10 minutes. Add chicken and juices; stir until heated through. Season to taste with salt and pepper. Cook pasta in salted water and then drain. Mix in sauce, 1 cup cheese and parsley. Serve, passing remaining cheese. Serves 4.

Jean Beaver

Penne all Arrabbiata

1 pound dry penne pasta

2 tablespoons olive oil

1 cup red onion, thinly sliced

2 teaspoons garlic, minced

6 ounces Genoa salami, cubed

1/2 teaspoon crushed red
  pepper flakes

2 (14.5 ounce) cans diced
  tomatoes with juice

1 tablespoon tomato paste

1 tablespoon brown sugar,
  packed

1 tablespoon balsamic vinegar

1/2 cup torn basil leaves

1/4 cup Parmesan cheese,
  grated

Arrabbiata means "angry" in Italian, and this pasta dish is spicy. Try buying salami in a 6 ounce chunk and remove rind.

Heat oil in a large sauté pan over medium-high heat. Add onion and sauté until soft and beginning to color, about 5 minutes. Add garlic, salami and red pepper flakes. Sauté until salami caramelizes, 5-7 minutes. Add tomatoes, tomato paste, brown sugar and vinegar. Reduce heat and simmer until slightly thickened, 10-15 minutes. Season with salt and pepper. Bring water to a boil and add pasta and cook until al dente. Drain pasta, reserving 1/4 cup liquid to thin sauce, if necessary. Transfer sauce to large shallow bowl and add drained pasta, torn basil and Parmesan to the sauce. Toss to coat and serve immediately. Sauce can be made ahead of time and refrigerated. Makes 6 cups sauce.

Jean Barclay

Penne alla Maria

Use fresh basil and oregano.

3 quarts water

4 tablespoons olive oil

6 cloves garlic, sliced

2 teaspoons basil

2 tablespoons sun-dried tomatoes

1 teaspoon oregano

1/4 cup white wine

1/2 cup consommé

1 pound penne rigate

4 cups fresh spinach, chopped

4 tablespoons pecorino cheese, grated

Bring water to a boil in large pot. Heat oil over medium-high heat in large sauté pan. Add garlic and sauté until golden in color. Add sun-dried tomatoes, oregano and basil. Continue to sauté for 30 seconds. Add white wine and simmer for 2 more minutes. Add consommé and simmer for 3 more minutes. Add penne to boiling water. Cook al dente. Drain well and return to pot. Pour sauce over pasta and mix well. Add chopped spinach and cook 3 minutes over medium heat, stirring constantly. Once pasta is well coated, remove from stove and place on the serving dish. Sprinkle with cheese. Serves 4-6.

Marie Fabiano

Penne alla Vodka

1/3 cup olive oil
1 pound prosciutto ham, cut
   in small pieces
3 cloves garlic, minced
1 tablespoon hot red pepper
   flakes

1 (24 ounce) can crushed
   tomatoes
16 ounces whipping cream
1/2 cup vodka
1/2 cup grated Parmesan cheese
1 pound penne pasta

Do not add salt—ham and cheese have enough salt.

In oil, brown prosciutto and garlic in a large, heavy saucepan. Add pepper flakes and tomatoes. Cook on low for 20 minutes. Add cream, vodka and cheese. Stir and heat. Serve over cooked penne pasta with additional cheese. Serves 4-6.

Char Macaluso

Penne with Broccoli Rabe

To clean up
hand grater:
Rub salad
oil on grater
before using.

1 pound broccoli rabe
1 pound penne pasta
3 tablespoons olive oil
1/3 cup sliced, pitted Kalamata
    olives
4 large garlic cloves, peeled
    and sliced

1/4 teaspoon crushed red
    pepper
Finely shredded Parmesan
    cheese
1/4 cup hot water

Wash broccoli rabe and cut into 2-inch pieces. Blanch rabe in large pot of salted water for 1-2 minutes. Remove, using slotted spoon, and drain. Bring water to a boil again. Add pasta and cook 10-12 minutes. Drain. Meanwhile, heat olive oil in large skillet over medium heat. Add olives, garlic and crushed red pepper. Stir and cook until garlic is tender, but not brown, about 2-3 minutes. Add broccoli rabe and 1/4 cup of hot water. Cook and stir for 3-5 minutes or until tender. Add drained pasta to skillet and toss. Mix well. Sprinkle with Parmesan cheese. Serves 6-8.

Rita Collins

Penne Pasta Marinara

1 pound penne pasta

1 tablespoon plus 1/2 teaspoon 100% pure Italian olive oil

2 cloves fresh chopped garlic

1 (12 ounce) can Progresso peeled Italian plum tomatoes with basil, mashed

Salt and pepper to taste

1 teaspoon fresh minced basil

1/3 cup dry white wine (optional)

1/4 cup freshly grated cheese (Parmesan or Asiago)

Few sprigs fresh mint

Cook penne pasta in large pot of boiling water with 1/2 teaspoon olive oil to keep pasta from sticking together. Cook pasta al dente. Drain. Warm olive oil and chopped garlic in Teflon pan. Add tomatoes, salt and pepper, fresh minced basil and dry white wine. Stir and allow to simmer, uncovered, for 20 minutes. Remove from stove and toss with penne pasta in large pasta bowl. Sprinkle with grated cheese and top with fresh mint. Serves 4-6.

Nancy Porter

Relax and enjoy this pasta dish with your favorite wine while listening to Andrea Bocelli.

Pink & Green Shrimp & Green Noodles

1/2 of 8 ounce package spinach noodles

2 pounds shrimp, peeled and deveined

1/2 cup clarified butter

1 can cream of mushroom soup

1 cup sour cream

1 cup mayonnaise

1 tablespoon chopped chives

1/2 teaspoon Dijon-style mustard

4 tablespoons dry sherry

1/2 cup sharp cheddar cheese, grated

Cook noodles as directed on package. Line 2-quart flat casserole with noodles. In large frying pan sauté shrimp in butter until pink and tender (about 5 minutes). Cover noodles with shrimp. Combine soup, sour cream, mayonnaise and chives. Add mustard and sherry. Pour sauce over shrimp and sprinkle cheese over all. Bake at 350° for 30 minutes or until cheese has melted and is bubbly. Serves 6.

Gail Webster-Patterson

Pizzaghetti

1 (16 ounce) box spaghetti
2 cups shredded mozzarella
   cheese
1 egg
1/4 cup milk
2 tablespoons parsley
1 pound ground beef or
   (1/2 pound ground beef and
   1/2 pound sausage)

1 small onion
1 large jar spaghetti sauce
1 can pizza sauce
Pepperoni

Great for a crowd. Can be made ahead of time and frozen.

Cook spaghetti and drain. While hot, toss with 1 cup mozzarella cheese, egg, milk and parsley. Bake for 20 minutes at 350° in 13"x20" baking dish sprayed with nonstick spray. Brown meat and onion. Add sauces. Pour meat, onion and sauces over baked spaghetti. Top with mozzarella cheese and pepperoni. Bake for 30 minutes at 350°; serve with garlic bread and tossed salad. Serves 10-12.

Pam Stallkamp

Puttanesca Sauce

3 cloves garlic, minced
1 small can sliced black olives
1 small jar stuffed green olives
4 tablespoons capers, drained
1/4 cup basil leaves, chopped
1/4 cup parsley, chopped
2 tablespoons olive oil
1 small sweet onion, chopped
2 large cans crushed tomatoes
1 pound spaghetti of your choice
1/4 cup sherry wine
1/2 cup grated cheese
1 can anchovies (they will melt completely)

Brown onions and garlic in oil in large, heavy saucepan. Add all other ingredients. Simmer for 45 minutes on low heat. Add 3/4 cup dry sherry. Heat and serve over spaghetti. Sprinkle with grated Parmesan cheese. Serves 4.

Char Macaluso

Ravioli with Walnut Sauce

1 1/2 cups shelled walnuts
3/4 cup olive oil
4 tablespoons butter
3/4 cup freshly grated Parmesan cheese
3 1/2 ounces heavy cream
Salt
24-36 ravioli stuffed with spinach and ricotta

Try different stuffed ravioli with same sauce. Serve on individual plates either as an appetizer or main course.

Chop nuts in a food processor. Add olive oil and butter. Add grated cheese, cream and salt to taste. Keep sauce warmed on low setting. Cook pasta according to directions, drain and serve with sauce.

Gayle Gordon Nering

Salmon Salad Shells

14 jumbo macaroni shells

1 (15 ounce) can salmon

1/2 cup mayonnaise

1/3 cup chopped green pepper

1/4 cup chopped onion

1/4 cup sweet pickle relish

2 teaspoons lemon juice

1/4 teaspoon salt

1/4 teaspoon pepper

1/8 teaspoon hot sauce

Lettuce

Cook pasta according to package directions. Drain and rinse with cold water; cover and chill. Combine next 9 ingredients; cover and chill. To serve, tear lettuce leaf into small pieces. Line each shell with lettuce. Spoon salmon into shells. Serve with fresh fruit. Serves 4-6.

Lori Sherman

Spaghetti Giovanni

8 ounce package spaghetti

2 tablespoons butter

1 small onion, minced

1 green pepper, chopped

1/2 cups mushrooms, sliced

2 cups canned tomatoes

3/4 teaspoon salt

3/4 teaspoon pepper

61/2 ounce crabmeat, canned

1/2 cup sour cream

1 cup shredded cheddar cheese

Following directions on package, cook spaghetti and drain. Melt butter in large skillet and sauté onion, green pepper and mushrooms for 10 minutes. Add tomatoes, salt and pepper; simmer covered for 10 minutes. Add crabmeat, sour cream and 1/2 cup cheddar cheese. Stir and place in 3-quart greased casserole bowl and sprinkle with 1/2 cup cheddar cheese. Bake uncovered at 375° for 20 minutes. Serves 6.

Nancy Near

Spaghetti Pie

1/2 pound angel hair pasta, drained and cooked

2 tablespoons olive oil

2 large eggs, beaten

1/2 cup plus 2 tablespoons grated Parmesan cheese

1 cup spaghetti sauce

1/2 cup shredded mozzarella cheese

1 (15 ounce) container ricotta cheese

Preheat oven to 350°. In a large bowl, toss hot angel hair pasta with olive oil. In small bowl combine eggs and 1/2 cup Parmesan cheese. Stir into spaghetti. Pour mixture into lightly greased 10-inch pie plate and form into "crust." Spread ricotta cheese evenly over crust but not quite to the edge. Top with spaghetti sauce. Bake uncovered for 25 minutes. Top with shredded mozzarella cheese. Bake for 5 minutes more or until cheese melts. Remove from oven and sprinkle with remaining 2 tablespoons Parmesan. Cool 10 minutes before cutting into wedges. Serves 6.

Jan Cancilla

Special Spaghetti Sauce

2 large green peppers, finely chopped
Olive oil
2 bay leaves
2 Bermuda onions, finely chopped
1 clove garlic (optional)

1 #3 can peeled tomatoes, seedless
1 small can tomato paste
1 or 1 1/2 pounds lean, top round, ground twice
1/2 bottle chili sauce

Sauce makes an unusual canapé served ice cold on crackers.

Sauté peppers in large skillet until tender, using pure olive oil. Add bay leaves, onions and garlic, if desired. Fry for 15 minutes, stirring constantly. Add tomatoes and stir until well blended. Add tomato paste, stir well and let cook about 20 minutes on low heat, just enough to simmer. Add ground round. Cook for about 1 1/2 hours, then add 1/2 bottle of chili sauce or more. Let moisture cook away, but be careful not to let ingredients dry out in cooking. Salt to taste during cooking. Remove the garlic. Makes 1 1/2 quarts of sauce.

Beverley McHugh

Spinach Lasagna

1 pound ricotta or small curd cottage cheese

11/2 cups shredded mozzarella cheese, divided

1 egg, beaten

1 package frozen, chopped spinach, thawed and drained

1 teaspoon salt

3/4 teaspoon oregano

1/8 teaspoon pepper

2 large jars spaghetti sauce

1/2 package lasagna noodles, uncooked

1 cup water

Mix ricotta, 1 cup mozzarella cheese, egg, spinach, salt, oregano and pepper. In greased 13"x9" pan, layer 1/2 cup spaghetti sauce, 1/3 noodles and 1/2 cheese and spinach mixture: repeat. Top with remaining noodles, then remaining sauce; sprinkle with remaining 1/2 cup mozzarella cheese. Pour water around edges. Cover with foil. Bake at 350° for 1 hour and 15 minutes. Let stand for 10 minutes before serving. Serves 8.

Carol Conant

Tortellini per Tutti

1/2 pint heavy whipping cream

2 tablespoons grated Parmesan cheese

1 clove garlic, crushed

Fresh cracked pepper to taste

Dash of salt

1/4 pound baby portabello mushrooms, washed and sliced

1 tablespoon olive oil

1 pound bag frozen tortellini (Rosetto's suggested)

Grated Parmesan cheese, to taste

Warm cream in small saucepan over low heat. Stir in 2 tablespoons Parmesan cheese. Add crushed garlic. Cook until thick and bubbly, stirring occasionally. Be careful not to overheat. Keep sauce warm while sautéing mushrooms in olive oil over medium heat. When the mushrooms are tender, drain the excess liquid and add mushrooms to cream sauce, continually heating. Boil at least 8 cups of water in large pot and add tortellini. Cook just until tortellini floats to the top. Drain and put back in large pan. Add sauce to tortellini and stir (no need to keep heating). Serve immediately. Serves 3.

Sally Stephenson

Veal Osso Buco
over Pasta

1/4 cup butter

2 tablespoons olive oil

4 veal shanks

Flour

1 (15 ounce) can cece beans

1/2 cup white wine

2 cups peeled, chopped
   tomatoes

1/4 pound mushrooms

1 large onion, chopped

3 cloves garlic, chopped

Fresh parsley or basil, chopped

Lemon rind, grated

In large roasting pan, sauté onion and 2 cloves garlic in butter and olive oil. Dust shanks in flour. Roast at 275° for 11/2 hours along with 1/2 the beans. Remove from oven, chill veal juices and defat. Place veal juice and onions in blender and pour over shanks in pan. Add tomatoes, 1/2 can of beans and mushrooms. Cover with white wine. Season to taste with salt and pepper. Roast at 275° for 1 hour and add mixture: 1 chopped garlic clove, parsley and lemon rind. Serve over pasta, risotto, or polenta. Serves 4.

Dorothy Pericola

Armenian Rice

1 cup rice (rinse until clean)
2 cups chicken broth
1 stick butter
4-6 buttons sliced garlic
1 cup broken vermicelli
1 bell pepper, sliced

1 small can mushrooms, stems and pieces, drained
1 small can sliced ripe olives, drained
1 can sliced water chestnuts, drained

Wash rice until clean. Place in 3-quart oblong Pyrex casserole and cover with chicken broth. Melt butter and cook garlic until golden. Remove garlic. Add vermicelli to butter. Cook vermicelli until dark brown. Add bell pepper (cut in large pieces), olives (halved), water chestnuts and mushrooms to casserole or rice and chicken broth. Stir until well mixed. Cover. Cook in preheated 350° oven for approximately 1 hour. May need to add 1/2 cup additional broth if it gets too dry. Rice should be done when broth is cooked away. Serves 12.

Mrs. James Robertson

Great with roast beef, pork loin, chicken, or fish.

Curried Rice

1 medium onion, diced
1/2 stick butter
2 teaspoons mild curry powder
1 1/2 cups long-grain rice

1 cup golden raisins
1 teaspoon garlic powder
1 tablespoon chicken bouillon
3 cups chicken broth

Sauté onion in butter until onion is transparent. Add curry powder to onion and stir. Mix in rice and stir until coated. Add remaining ingredients. Bring to a boil and reduce heat. Cook uncovered until broth is absorbed.

Joanne Rainey Slaughter

Gilda's Rice

Roasted peanuts may be used instead of cashews, and white raisins may be substituted for the currants.

1/2 cup currants
1 bunch chopped scallions
1 red pepper, chopped
1 yellow pepper, chopped
1/2 tin honey roasted cashews
1 package frozen baby peas
2 boxes Uncle Ben's white
   wild rice

Dressing:
1/4 cup honey
1/4 cup white wine vinegar
1/4 cup vegetable oil
2 teaspoons curry powder

Cook rice according to package directions. Add first 6 items to rice, which has cooled. Then mix last 4 ingredients to make the dressing. Add to rice mixture. Serves 10.

Jeri Bowman

Green Chili/Cheese Rice Casserole

3/4 pound Monteray Jack cheese, sliced

2 (4 ounce) cans green chilies, chopped

3 cups sour cream, salted

3 cups cooked rice, Basmati or regular white

1/2-1 cup cheddar cheese, grated

Vegetable oil

Basmati gives extra flavor, but any white rice can be used.

In a greased 11/2-quart casserole, place ingredients in layers as follows: Layer 1 cup of rice. Layer with 11/2 cups cream mixture (sour cream with green chilies), strips of cheese, 1 cup rice; cream mixture, cheese strips, ending with rice on top. Bake covered 1/2 hour at 350°. During last 10 minutes, uncover and sprinkle grated cheddar on top. Continue baking until cheese melts. Serves 4.

Lynn Schneider

Hawaiian Fried Rice

8-10 slices bacon
10-12 small green onions
1/2 cup raw rice, cooked the
    day before and refrigerated
1/4 cup cocktail peanuts, diced
1 hard-boiled egg

2 tablespoons coconut flakes
2-4 tablespoons Kikkoman
    teriyaki marinade
2 slices canned pineapple,
    crushed (optional)

Cut bacon in small pieces and sauté in medium frying pan. Add diced green onions and sauté slightly. Turn heat off. Add refrigerated rice (or 1 cup leftover rice) and rest of ingredients. Add marinade to moisten. Serve warmed. Serves 4.

Margaret Warfield

Rice Chantilly

3 cups cooked rice
1/2 to 1 cup sour cream
1 teaspoon salt

1 cup grated sharp cheddar
    cheese
1-2 dashes cayenne pepper

Combine rice, sour cream, salt, cayenne pepper and 1/2 cup cheese. Spoon into buttered shallow 1-quart baking dish. Top with remaining cheese. Bake at 350° for 20 minutes. Serves 4.

Mary Jo Lombardi

Rice & Noodle Casserole

1/2 pound butter or margarine
1/2 pound uncooked very fine noodles
2 cups uncooked instant rice
2 cans onion soup

2 cans chicken broth
1 teaspoon soy sauce
1 cup water
8 ounces canned sliced water chestnuts, drained

In large pot, melt butter or margarine. Add noodles. Cook until lightly browned, stirring frequently. Add remaining ingredients. Mix well. Pour everything into greased 3-quart uncovered casserole. Bake in preheated oven at 350° for 45 minutes. Serves 12-14.

Joyce Kelly

Risotto with Mushrooms & Pea Pods

1/4 pound fresh mushrooms, sliced

4 green onions, diced

1/4 cup olive oil

1 cup Arborio (Italian rice)

1/4 cup dry white wine

4 cups warm chicken broth, divided

1/4 pound shelled, deveined medium shrimp

1/4 cup grated Parmesan cheese

1/4 cup grated mozzarella cheese

1/4 cup julienned pea pods, blanched

In a large skillet, sauté mushrooms and green onions for 5 minutes in oil. Add rice. Cook for 2 minutes; do not let burn. Add wine and 1/3 cup chicken broth, simmering slowly and stirring frequently until broth is almost absorbed. Add 1/3 cup broth. Repeat procedure until 1/3 cup broth remains, about 30 minutes. Add shrimp and remaining 1/3 cup broth. Simmer for 5 minutes. Remove from heat and stir in cheese and pea pods. Serves 4.

Joyce Kelly

Saffron Rice

2 tablespoons oil

3 tablespoons chopped onion

1 1/2 cups long-grain rice

3 cups water or chicken stock and water

1 tablespoon salt

1/8 tablespoon saffron threads

2 tablespoons pine nuts

3 tablespoons finely chopped parsley

Heat oil in heavy saucepan. Add onions, stirring frequently (until soft—not brown) for about 5 minutes. Pour in rice and stir to coat well with oil. Add water or stock and water, salt and saffron. Bring to a boil while stirring. Cover saucepan; reduce heat and simmer for 20 minutes or until liquid is absorbed and rice is cooked. Add pine nuts and parsley. Fluff rice with fork. Taste for seasoning. Serves 6.

Nina Foster

Swedish Rice

1 cup long-grain rice (not converted)

4-6 cups 1% or 2% milk

1/3 cup sugar

1 scant teaspoon cinnamon

Mix rice, 4 cups of milk and sugar in double broiler. Cook covered over simmering water until rice is tender and milk is absorbed (about 1 1/4 hours). Stir occasionally. Add milk as necessary. Remove from heat and add cinnamon. Serve hot or cold with toppings of fruit, raisins, or chopped nuts if desired. Can be made day ahead of time. Cover tightly in refrigerator. To serve add more milk for creamy consistency. Gently reheat in microwave. Serve 4-6.

Joyce Kelly

Wild Rice

1 (8 ounce) package of wild rice

3 cups boiling water

Preheat oven to 500°. Wash wild rice and drain. Place in 11/2 quart casserole dish. Pour over 3 cups of boiling water. TURN OFF THE OVEN! Place the casserole dish in the oven overnight or for at least 8 hours. DO NOT PEEK! Next day mix the following into the rice:

1/2 cup chopped red onion

3/4 cups dried cranberries

1/4 cups coarsely chopped walnuts

1/3 cup balsamic vinegar

21/2 tablespoons sugar

3/4 cup olive oil

Chill thoroughly. May be made a day ahead as it gets better as it marinates together. Serves 10-14.

Fran Gilbert

Meat

Barbecued Baby Back Ribs

Beef Barbecue Sloppy Joes

Beef En Wine Casserole

Beef Stroganoff

Boeuf Bourguignon

Braised Veal

Broiled Flank Steak

Cold Marinated Tenderloin

Corned Beef with Mustard Sauce

Coté de Veau Moutard

Daven Haven Ham Loaf

Filet Mignon en Marinade

Grilled Pork Chops

Ground Beef & Wild Rice Casserole

Lamb Chops with Mint

Lois' Wine Brisket Delight

Marinated Pork Tenderloin with Pineapple Salsa

Marinated Rack of Lamb

Mimi's Ribs

Mustard Glazed Spareribs

Pork Cutlets

Roast Veal with Honey, Mustard & Rosemary

Super Veal Chops

Sweet & Sour Meatballs

Veal Rolls Sicily

Veal Schnitzel

Barbecued Baby Back Ribs

4 slabs of baby back ribs

Sauce:
1 cup ketchup
1 cup chili sauce
2/3 cup honey
2 tablespoons vinegar
2 tablespoons dark molasses
2 tablespoons Worcestershire sauce
4 teaspoons prepared mustard
1 teaspoon paprika
1/2 teaspoon garlic powder
1/4 teaspoon cayenne pepper

Place ribs in a 9"x13" baking pan ribs side up and bake in preheated 250° oven for 3 hours. Then turn the ribs over and bake for 1 more hour. Then pour 1/3 of the sauce over the ribs and bake 1 more hour. Turn the ribs over again and pour 1/3-2/3 of the sauce over the ribs and bake for 1 more hour (6 hours in all). Serves 4-6.

Mary Gill Teschner

Beef Barbecue Sloppy Joes

3 1/2 pounds ground beef
1 pint sweet pickle relish
1 pint ketchup
1 pint chili sauce
2 stalks celery, chopped fine
4 medium onions, chopped fine
1 green pepper
Salt and pepper to taste

Brown meat, draining fat. Add all other ingredients. Simmer 1 hour. Serve on hamburger buns. Serves 40.

Jean Barclay

meat

Slow, low temperature baking is the most helpful hint to tender, delicious barbecued baby back ribs. Ribs can be frozen for later use.

Make 1 or 2 days ahead. Freezes well.

Beef En Wine Casserole

Simple and
tasty!

2 pounds boneless London
broil, cut into cubes

12 small white onions, fresh
or frozen

1 package frozen peas

5 carrots, quartered
(lengthwise)

1 (14 ounce) can chopped
tomatoes

1 teaspoon salt

1/4 teaspoon pepper

1 tablespoon Worcestershire
sauce

1/2 cup dry bread crumbs

1/4 cup minute tapioca

1 clove garlic, peeled and
quartered

1 package sliced fresh
mushrooms

1 cup red wine

Put all ingredients in 2 1/2-3 quart casserole and
cover. Bake in a very slow oven at 250° for 4-5 hours
until carrots are tender. Stir once or twice. Serves 8.

Bobbie Juster

Beef Stroganoff

2 pounds beef filet or flank
steak

2 tablespoons flour

1 1/2 sticks butter

1 cup beef stock

1/2 pound fresh mushrooms,
sliced

1 small can Italian tomatoes

1/2 pint sour cream

1 cup chopped onion

2 tablespoons capers

Salt and pepper to taste

Slice filet or flank steak into strips. Chill in refrigerator for 2 hours. Melt 1 stick of butter in frying pan, and sauté onion at high heat until soft. Add meat strips and fry until golden brown. Season with salt and pepper. Melt 2 tablespoons butter in pan and sauté mushrooms until tender and golden. Remove to a bowl with beef and onion mixture. In the same pan, melt 2 tablespoons butter and blend in flour until smooth. Add beef stock and continue cooking until well blended. Cool. When cool, alternately add tomatoes and the sour cream. When blended, add beef, onion, mushroom mixture and capers. Serves 8-10.

Sue Ann Furbee

May add 3 tablespoons Worcestershire sauce and 2 teaspoons paprika to roux to enhance flavor. Can be served with buttered poppyseed noodles.

Boeuf Bourguignon

5 medium onions, sliced

4 tablespoons cooking oil

2 pounds lean beef, cut in
  1-inch cubes

1/4 teaspoon thyme

1/2 cup beef bouillon

1 cup dry red wine

1/2 pound fresh mushrooms,
  sliced

11/2 teaspoons salt

1/2 teaspoon pepper

Cook onions in oil in heavy skillet until tender.
Remove and place in another dish. In the same pan,
sauté beef until brown. Sprinkle with flour and seasonings. Add bouillon and wine. Stir well and simmer
slowly for 11/2-2 hours. Add additional bouillon and
wine if necessary, in order to keep beef barely covered. Add onions and mushrooms and cook 30 minutes longer, stirring occasionally. Sauce should be
thick and dark brown. Serves 6.

Marion Gamble

Braised Veal

4 pounds boned and tied roast of veal (loin, leg, or shoulder)

2 tablespoons olive oil

2 tablespoons butter

1 cup bourbon whiskey or brandy

Bay leaf, parsley, thyme (bouquet garni)

1/2 cup Dijon mustard

2 teaspoons powdered ginger

1 cup light brown sugar

2 cups or more veal or chicken broth

24 prunes poached in Port wine (to cover)

2 tablespoons chopped parsley

Meat in the gravy tastes even better the next day. Freezes well.

Preheat oven to 375°. Brown veal in oil and butter in a Dutch oven or skillet. Turn meat to brown on all sides. Pour on whiskey. Add the bouquet garni (3-4 springs fresh parsley, 1 bay leaf and 1 large sprig of fresh thyme or 1 teaspoon dry thyme) to the pot. Pour mixture of mustard, ginger and sugar all over meat. Cover pan and cook in oven for 45 minutes. Add broth and continue cooking for 11/4 hours or until meat feels almost tender. Add prunes with the wine to the pot and cook for 20 minutes. Remove meat onto a board. Allow to rest for 5 minutes. Carve into 3/4-inch slices. Place on a heated platter and spoon sauce over all. Place prunes on the side for garnish. Sprinkle just a touch of parsley down the center. Serves 6.

Marie Hersh

Broiled Flank Steak

You may substitute shallots or onions for the scallions.

2 pounds or more flank steak
4 sliced scallions
2 tablespoons olive oil

2 tablespoons lemon juice
1/4 teaspoon powdered thyme
Pepper to taste

Score steak on both sides. Mix remaining ingredients together. Place meat in broiling pan without rack. Pour 1/2 of the marinade over it, turn, and pour remaining 1/2 marinade over it. Cover with plastic wrap and refrigerate turning occasionally—30 minutes or overnight. Broil on high to desired doneness. Best served rare, carved on slant. Serves 6.

Lynn Cole

Cold Marinated Tenderloin

Perfect for a cocktail buffet.

3-4 pounds beef tenderloin

Marinade:
1/2 cup soy sauce
6 tablespoons honey

4 tablespoons vinegar
3 teaspoons garlic powder
3 teaspoons ground ginger
1 1/2 cups salad oil
2 green onions, chopped

Combine soy sauce, honey, vinegar, garlic powder, ginger, oil and onions. Place meat in a shallow glass pan and cover with marinade. Refrigerate for at least 12 hours. Bring meat to room temperature. Grill for 20-25 minutes, basting with marinade. Refrigerate overnight, slice thin and serve. Serves 6-8.

Mary Nash

Corned Beef with Mustard Sauce

6 pounds corned beef brisket

2 cloves garlic

4 bay leaves

10 whole cloves

1/3 cup brown sugar, packed

1 teaspoon prepared mustard

1/3 cup ketchup

3 tablespoons vinegar

3 tablespoons water

Cover corned beef with water and simmer with garlic and bay leaves 3-4 hours or until tender. Cool in the liquid. Drain. Stud the fat side with cloves. Blend remaining ingredients and spread over meat. Bake uncovered at 275° about an hour, basting occasionally with the sauce. Slice meat very thin across the grain. Serves 12.

Jean Barclay

Meat can be cooked the day before serving and kept in liquid until baking.

Coté de Veau Moutard

6 tablespoons shallots,
  chopped fine

1 1/2 pound veal scallopini

Flour to coat

3 tablespoons olive oil

1 cup dry white wine

2 heaping teaspoons Dijon
  mustard

5 tablespoons butter

Salt and pepper to taste

1/2 cup whipping cream

Sauté shallots in 2 tablespoons butter until soft. Set aside. Coat veal with flour. Heat remaining butter and olive oil. Sauté veal. Place veal in an ovenproof dish at 175° to keep warm. Add wine to a skillet and reduce to a syrupy consistency. Add shallots and mustard. Slowly add cream. Remove from heat and pour over veal. Serves 6.

Carolyn Sauve

Daven Haven Ham Loaf

1 cup milk

1 cup bread crumbs

2 slightly beaten eggs

2 pounds lean ground smoked
ham

11/2 pounds lean ground pork

Brown Sugar Glaze:

3/4 cup brown sugar

1/4 cup water

2 teaspoons dry mustard

1/4 cup vinegar

Horseradish Sauce:

1/4 cup horseradish

11/2 tablespoons vinegar

1 tablespoon prepared
mustard

1/2 teaspoon salt

Dash of paprika

4 drops Worcestershire sauce

1/2 cup whipping cream
(whipped)

Combine first 5 ingredients well. Pack in loaf pan
and then invert onto shallow baking pan. Combine
ingredients for brown sugar glaze in small saucepan.
Simmer for a few minutes then pour over the ham loaf.
Baste with glaze 3-4 times while baking for 1 1/2 hours
in preheated 350° oven. Serve with special horseradish
sauce: add all ingredients to whipping cream and serve
in hollowed-out cucumbers. Serves 6-8.

Peggy Hanson

Filet Mignon
en Marinade

8 (6 ounce) filet mignon
2 cloves garlic, crushed
2 tablespoons brandy
3 tablespoons flour
2 teaspoons tomato paste
3/4 cup red wine

11/2 cups beef broth
1/4 teaspoon Worcestershire
   sauce
2 tablespoons currant jelly
1/2 pound mushrooms, sliced
Butter or margarine

Day ahead: Mix half the garlic with seasoned salt
and pepper and rub into steaks. Brown steaks over
high heat in butter. Put steaks in 9"x13" pan. Add
more butter and brandy to frying pan. Stir in flour
and reduce heat. Add the rest of the garlic and tomato paste, wine, broth and cook 10 minutes. Add
Worcestershire sauce, jelly and mushrooms (can add
more wine). Cool and pour over steaks. Cover with
plastic wrap and refrigerate overnight.

Next Day: Bring to room temperature. Preheat
oven to 400°. Bake uncovered 16-20 minutes for
medium/rare and 20-25 minutes for medium/well.
Serve with sauce. Serves 8.

Kay Wing

Grilled Pork Chops

1/3 cup Dijon mustard

1/4 cup brown sugar

1 tablespoon bottled steak sauce

4 boneless pork chops, 1-inch thick

8 peach halves

2 tablespoons brown sugar

1 tablespoon water

Combine mustard, 1/4 cup brown sugar and steak sauce. Place pork chops in mix and coat well. Grill over medium heat about 10-12 minutes, turning and brushing with sauce occasionally. Place on dinner plates. Glaze: Mix together 2 tablespoons brown sugar and water. Place 8 peach halves on grill, brush with glaze and grill 5-8 minutes, turning occasionally and brushing with glaze until hot and lightly browned. Serves 4.

Billie Stevens

Ground Beef & Wild Rice Casserole

An old favorite!

1 package Uncle Ben's Wild Rice Mix

3 cups boiling water

6 tablespoons chopped onion

11/2 pounds ground beef

2 small cans sliced mushrooms

2 cans mushroom soup

2 beef bouillon cubes dissolved in 1 cup hot water

3/4-1 teaspoon garlic salt

3/4 cup chopped celery

Pepper to taste

1 bay leaf

1/2 cup slivered almonds

Place rice mix and seasoning from packet in a bowl and pour over 3 cups boiling water. Let this sit for 15 minutes and then drain. Brown the onions and ground beef. Add to the rice mixture. Add the mushrooms and the soup. Gradually add the dissolved bouillon and mix in the garlic salt, chopped celery and pepper to taste. Crumble in the bay leaf and add the almonds. Cover and refrigerate in 21/2 quart casserole or 9"x13" pan overnight or for at least 2 hours. Bake covered for 11/2 hours at 350°. Serves 8-10.

Grace Seitz

Lamb Chops with Mint

4 loin lamb chops, 1-11/2
  inches thick

Salt and pepper, freshly ground

2 tablespoons soy sauce

1/4 cup crème de menthe

1 tablespoon fresh mint,
  chopped

For this recipe, serve with cabernet wine.

Brown chops in olive oil or lamb fat (cut from edges of chops if possible) 5 minutes on each side or to desired doneness. Season with salt and pepper. Place on heated platter and keep warm in 180° oven. Pour off all but 1 teaspoon or so of fat. If there is no fat left in the sauté pan, it is all right to omit it. Add soy sauce and crème de menthe to pan, warm it, pour it over each chop and sprinkle with chopped fresh mint for garnish. Serves 4.

Mickey Baumgartner

Lois' Wine Brisket Delight

1 large package of mushrooms

2 cans tomato soup

2 cans mushroom soup

3-4 pounds brisket

1 package onion soup

1/2 cup water

1/2 cup red wine

Lowrey salt, season lightly

Garlic salt, season lightly

8 small potatoes

8 large carrots, cut into thirds

Preheat oven to 350°. Combine all the above ingredients. Place in heavy roasting pot with cover. Cover roasting pot and cook at 350° for 31/2-4 hours. Serves 8.

Lois Lipnik

Marinated Pork Tenderloin with Pineapple Salsa

2 tablespoons salt
1 tablespoon allspice
2 teaspoons cayenne pepper
21/2 pounds pork tenderloin
1 tablespoon canola oil
1/4 cup chopped fresh mint, parsley, or cilantro

Pineapple Salsa:
11/2 cups diced fresh pineapple

2-3 plum tomatoes, seeded and diced
1 avocado, diced
1/2 cup Vidalia onion
2 tablespoons lemon
1/4 tablespoon orange juice
2 tablespoons olive oil
1/4 cup chopped fresh mint, parsley or cilantro
Salt and pepper

Combine salt, allspice and pepper and rub on tenderloins. Brown each in oil in fry pan over medium heat, one at a time. Transfer to large roasting pan. Bake for 20-25 minutes or to 155° on meat thermometer. Let stand for 5-10 minutes. Arrange on a platter. Garnish with mint, parsley, or cilantro. Serve with pineapple salsa. For the pineapple salsa, combine all ingredients in small serving bowl. Serves 6.

Nina Foster

Marinated Rack
of Lamb

4 (6-8 rib) lamb rib roasts

Marinade:
1 cup dry, white vermouth
1 cup Dale's seasoning sauce

3 tablespoons garlic powder
2 tablespoons dry Italian
   seasoning
Fresh parsley sprigs for
   garnish

Place lamb in a large shallow dish or large, heavy-duty zip-top plastic bag. Combine next 4 ingredients. Pour 1 cup marinade mixture over lamb. Reserve remaining marinade mixture. Refrigerate. Cover dish or seal bags and refrigerate for 8 hours, turning lamb frequently. Remove meat from marinade. Place lamb, fat side up, on a rack in a shallow roasting pan. Bake at 325° for 1 hour and 15 minutes or until a meat thermometer registers 150° (medium-rare), basting often with reserved marinade. Garnish with parsley, if desired. Serves 12.

Judie Grossman

One cup of any brand of soy sauce-based marinade may be substituted. Remove lamb from oven at 155° (on meat thermometer) for more well-done meat. The internal temperature will climb about 5° upon standing.

Mimi's Ribs

Meat will fall right off the bone!

1 rack of baby-back ribs

Honey Barbecue Sauce:
1 small onion, chopped
2 cloves garlic, chopped

11/2 cups ketchup
2 tablespoons white vinegar
1 cup Naples Finest Honey
1 teaspoon yellow mustard
1/2 teaspoon pepper

Wash, salt and pepper ribs. Place in flat pan and cook in oven for 45 minutes at 400°. Take out of oven, cover with honey barbecue sauce, add 1 cup of water, and cover tightly with foil. Cook for 60 minutes at 350°. For honey barbecue sauce, blend ingredients above and heat in medium saucepan. Bring to a boil and pour over ribs. Serves 2.

Tom, Kirsten & Mary May

Mustard Glazed Spareribs

5 pounds baby back pork ribs

Marinade:
11/2 cups light soy sauce
21/2 cups pineapple juice
11/2 cups honey
1/2 cup Dijon mustard

Glaze:
1 cup honey
1/2 cup Dijon mustard

Ribs take 3 days to prepare. Clean and marinate first day; bake and cool 2nd day; grill or bake and eat 3rd day.

Combine the marinade and mix well in large glass or nonreactive bowl. Clean ribs by removing layer of skin on inside of ribs, and wash ribs well in cold water. Place ribs in bowl of marinade and marinate 24 hours. Turn ribs periodically. Preheat oven to 350°. Bake ribs in heavy covered pan with 2 cups of marinade and bake for 21/2-3 hours. Ribs are done when they pull away from the bone when pulled gently with a fork. Cool ribs to room temperature. Refrigerate ribs for 8-24 hours. Cut ribs into individual pieces. Glaze: Combine 1 cup honey and 1/2 cup Dijon mustard. Baste ribs with glaze and grill on a barbecue grill or bake at 350° until heated through–about 15 minutes. Makes 4 dinner servings or 12 appetizer servings.

Herbert Rowe

Pork Cutlets

1/3 cup maple syrup

1 tablespoon brown sugar

1/4 teaspoon salt

1/4 teaspoon pepper

1/4 cup dry bread crumbs

4 (4 ounce) pork cutlets

2 teaspoons olive oil

1/2 cup apple cider

2 medium Golden Delicious apples

2 tablespoons chopped fresh parsley

Combine first 4 ingredients in a small bowl; stir well, set aside. Place crumbs in plastic bag. Add pork and shake until coated with crumbs. Heat oil in non-stick skillet over medium heat. Add pork and cook until golden brown on each side. Add cider and apple wedges; bring to a boil. Reduce heat and simmer uncovered for 10 minutes or until pork is done. Add maple syrup mixture and cook 5 minutes until thick and syrupy. Sprinkle with parsley. Serves 4.

Doris Rosenberg

Roast Veal with Honey, Mustard & Rosemary

3 pound veal roast

3 tablespoons Dijon mustard

1 tablespoon honey

1 teaspoon garlic, minced

1 tablespoon fresh rosemary

1 teaspoon butter

1 cup chicken stock

Blend mustard, honey, garlic, and rosemary in a small bowl. After scoring veal, brush with marinade. Let stand for 1/2 hour. Preheat oven to 400°. Put veal in roasting pan. Pour 1/2 cup chicken stock in bottom of pan. Rub butter on top of veal roast and roast for 11/2 hours, basting frequently. Add more stock if necessary. Make gravy with pan drippings. Serves 6-8.

Carolyn Sauve

Super Veal Chops

4 veal chops, 11/4 inch thick
2 tablespoons soy sauce
2 tablespoons oil
2 tablespoons grainy Dijon
  mustard
1 tablespoon minced fresh
  ginger or 1 teaspoon dried
  ginger

2 cloves garlic, crushed
1/3 cup green onion, diced
1/4 cup dry white wine
Salt and freshly ground pepper
  to taste

Mix all ingredients in plastic bag. Add chops; turn to coat. Marinate at room temperature for 2 hours or up to 24 hours in refrigerator. Preheat broiler or grill on high. Drain marinade into saucepan. Salt and pepper chops. Grill chops 4-5 minutes on each side. While chops are grilling, bring marinade to a boil and simmer until chops are done. Spoon sauce over cooked chops. Serves 4.

Sandra Roth

Sweet & Sour Meatballs

1 pound ground lean beef
1 egg
1 tablespoon cornstarch
2 tablespoons finely chopped onion
1 tablespoon oil
1 (20 ounce) can cubed pineapple
3 tablespoons cornstarch
1 tablespoon soy sauce
3 tablespoons vinegar
1/2 cup sugar
6 tablespoons water
1 green pepper sliced, if desired
Salt to taste

Mix beef, egg, cornstarch and onion and form into 1-inch meatballs and brown slightly in 1 tablespoon oil. Drain pineapple and warm over low heat. Mix 3 tablespoons cornstarch, soy sauce, vinegar, sugar and water. Gradually add to warm juice and cook until it thickens, stirring constantly. Can be made ahead of time at this point. Reheat and add meatballs, pineapple and green pepper and serve hot from a chafing dish. Top with red maraschino cherries, if desired. Serves 6-8 for dinner and 15+ for hors d'oeuvres.

Suzie Lipp

Veal Rolls Sicily

1 1/2 pounds of veal scallopini
1/2 pound prosciutto ham, sliced
1 cup seasoned bread crumbs
1 cup grated Parmesan cheese
2 cloves minced garlic
1 tablespoon basil
1 tablespoon oregano leaves
1 (3 ounce) bottle pine nuts, finely chopped
1/2 cup olive oil
1 pound mushrooms, sliced
1 cup dry white wine
Salt and pepper to taste

Lay thin scallopini pieces on cutting board. Put layer of proscuitto on each piece of veal. Roll up and secure with string. Mix bread crumbs, cheese, garlic, herbs and pine nuts; spread over veal. Brown meat rolls in olive oil in frying pan. Layer meat rolls, mushrooms and white wine in 2-quart casserole with lid. Bake at 350° for 1 1/2 hours. Serves 4-6.

Char Macaluso

Veal Schnitzel

4 thin veal cutlets
1 teaspoon salt
1/4 teaspoon pepper
1/2 cup flour
1 egg, beaten
2 tablespoons milk
2/4 cup dry bread crumbs
1/4 pound butter

Beat or tenderize cutlets; season with salt and pepper. Dip into flour, then combine egg and milk. Moisten veal with egg mixture; roll into bread crumbs. Fry in butter only turning once, until golden brown. Cover and cook for 5 minutes. Serves 4.

Marcia Kelley

Seafood

Angel Hair Pasta with Scallops, Hazelnuts & Basil
Around the World Scampi
Baked Grouper Bites with Banana Salsa
Baked Oysters with Sherry
Baked Salmon with Tarragon Peppercorn Cream Sauce
Baked Shrimp with Sherry
Brown Sugar Salmon
Buffet Crab
Crab Soufflé
Crispy Fish Fillets
Easy Baked Scallops
Easy Hot Weather Salmon Mousse
El Greco's Shrimp
Elegant Poached Salmon
Fillet of Sole Rive Gauche
Florida Shrimp with Pasta & Feta
Fresh Salmon in Vinaigrette
Grilled Fillet of Salmon
Grilled Swordfish
Grouper Tropicale
Grouper Au Gratin
Lobster Thermidor
Lu's Scallop Castine
Maine Lobster Newburg
Marinated Scallops
Maryland Lady Crab Cakes
Orange & Bourbon Salmon
Parmesan Catfish
Parmesan Sole
Roast Salmon with Asparagus
Salmon en Croute
Salmon Florentine
Scalloped Oysters
Scallops with Grand Marnier
Sebastian's Scallops Oregano
Shrimp & Cheese Soufflé
Shrimp Curry with Egg Noodles
Shrimp & Feta Cheese over Angel Hair Pasta
Shrimp de Jonghe
Shrimp & Sun-Dried Tomatoes with Linguine
South Carolina Shrimp Creole
Spicy Baked Shrimp
Spicy Sautéed Fish with Olives & Cherry Tomatoes
Szechwan Shrimp
Tropical Lemon Sole

Angel Hair Pasta with Scallops, Hazelnuts & Basil

5 tablespoons butter

1 cup shallots, chopped fine

4 thin slices prosciutto, cut into thin strips

21/2 tablespoons fresh basil, minced

1 cup whipping cream

16 ounces angel hair pasta

12 ounces scallops

1/4 cup hazelnuts, chopped

3 tablespoons snipped fresh chives

Salt and pepper

Melt 4 tablespoons butter in skillet over medium-low heat. Add shallots and 1/2 the prosciutto until shallots are transparent (about 6 minutes). Add basil and cook 2 minutes. Pour in cream and reduce by 1/4, about 10 minutes. Season with salt and pepper. Cook pasta. Bring cream mixture to gentle simmer. Add scallops and cook until opaque about 2 minutes. Drain pasta and mix with 1 tablespoon butter. Arrange pasta in nests on plates. Spoon scallop mixture in center of nests. Sprinkle with nuts and chives. Place remaining prosciutto strips atop scallops. Serve immediately. Serves 4.

Carolyn Sauve

Around the World Scampi

An easy "do-ahead" gourmet dish.

4 strips of bacon
1 garlic clove, minced
1 onion chopped fine
1 cup vermouth
1 cup beef bouillon
2 cups stewed tomatoes

Salt
Pepper
Basil or Tabasco sauce
1 cup uncooked long grain rice
1 pound cooked shrimp,
   shelled and deveined

Cut bacon into 1/2-inch pieces and sauté. Add garlic and onion and cook until transparent. Add wine, broth, tomatoes and seasonings. Simmer for 10 minutes. Add rice and cook for 20 minutes. Add shrimp and cook for 5 more minutes, or until shrimp is done. Serves 4-6.

Delores Lyon

Baked Grouper Bites with Banana Salsa

1 1/2 cups crushed potato chips
1/4 cup grated Parmesan cheese
1 teaspoon ground thyme
1 pound grouper filets, cut
   into strips
1/4 cup milk

Banana Salsa:
1/2 cup chopped green bell
   pepper
1/2 cup chopped red bell
   pepper

3 green onions, chopped
1 tablespoon chopped cilantro
1 small jalapeño, seeded and
   chopped (optional)
2 tablespoons light brown sugar
3 tablespoons fresh lime juice
1 tablespoon vegetable oil
1/4 teaspoon salt
1/4 teaspoon pepper
2 medium bananas, chopped

For the grouper, mix the potato chips, cheese and thyme in a shallow dish. Dip the fish into the milk and then into the potato chip mixture, coating well. Arrange in a single layer in a greased baking dish. Bake at 500° for 8-10 minutes or until cooked through. Serve with banana salsa. For the salsa, combine the bell peppers, green onion, cilantro, jalapeño, brown sugar, lime juice, oil, salt and pepper in a large bowl and mix well. Add the bananas and mix gently. Chill covered for 3 hours or longer. Serves 4.

Joan Shipman

Baked Oysters
with Sherry

Serve with a
glass of
Manzanilla
sherry wine,
if desired.

1 pint oysters, shelled

11/2 cups crushed Ritz
   crackers

7 tablespoons butter

2 teaspoons fresh lemon juice

Salt and pepper to taste

2/3 cup heavy cream

1 tablespoon Manzanilla sherry
   or other dry sherry

1/4 teaspoon Worcestershire
   sauce

Drain oysters and reserve juice (about 1/2 cup or if
not sufficient use clam juice). Combine crackers, butter, lemon juice, salt and pepper. Sprinkle 1/3 crumb
mixture in bottom of 3-cup shallow baking dish. Add
1/3 of oysters over crumbs. Sprinkle another 1/3 of
crumb mixture over oysters. Add remaining oysters.
Whisk cream, sherry, reserved oyster juice and
Worcestershire sauce and pour over oysters. Sprinkle
with remaining crumbs. Bake at 350° for about 40
minutes. Serve hot. Serves 6.

Mickey Baumgartner

Baked Salmon with Tarragon Peppercorn Cream Sauce

8 salmon fillets, boned and skinless

3 tablespoons olive oil or melted butter

4 tablespoons olive oil or butter

1 cup mushrooms, sliced

1 medium tomato

2 teaspoons green peppercorns

4 tablespoons fresh tarragon, no stems

11/2 cups whipping cream

Salt and pepper to taste

Oil a large baking pan, enough to hold salmon fillets. Place fillets in pan, brush with butter or oil and bake in a preheated oven at 450° for 8-10 minutes. Place 4 tablespoons butter/oil in large sauté pan. Add mushrooms and lightly sauté (about 2 minutes). Add peeled and chopped tomato, green peppercorns and tarragon; warm these ingredients for about 1 minute. Add cream and reduce heat for 3-5 minutes to desired consistency. Add salt and pepper to taste. Pour over salmon. Serves 8.

Dottie Brennan

Baked Shrimp
with Sherry

11/2 pounds large shrimp, cooked, shelled and deveined

1/2 cup unsalted butter, softened

2 tablespoons medium dry sherry

1/2 cup dry bread crumbs

1/4 cup finely chopped fresh parsley

Dash of garlic salt

1/4 cup sliced almonds, toasted

Preheat oven to 400°. Wash and pat shrimp dry. Arrange in 1 layer in buttered 1-quart gratin dish or any ovenproof dish. Mix together butter, sherry, bread crumbs, parsley, garlic salt and pepper to taste. Dot shrimp with crumb mixture and sprinkle with toasted almonds. Bake until warmed through and crumb mixture is lightly brown, about 10 minutes. Serves 4.

Leslie Branda

Brown Sugar Salmon

6 salmon steaks or 1 1/2
    pound fillet (1 inch thick)
Pam Cooking spray

Marinade:
1/2 cup brown sugar

4 tablespoons melted butter
3 tablespoons Kikkoman soy
    sauce
2 tablespoons lemon juice
2 tablespoons white wine or
    water

Mix marinade in bowl. Prepare 8"x8" or 9"x 9" baking pan with foil. Spray Pam on pan; place salmon in pan and pour marinade over it. Place a large piece of foil over pan to cover sides. Chill in refrigerator 30 minutes to 6 hours. Uncover pan and place in 400° oven. Bake 15-20 minutes until fish is done. Baste every 5 minutes. Do not turn fish. Serve immediately. Serves 6.

Isabelle Staffeldt

Cooking time for fish is 10 minutes per inch. You may double the marinade, as the sauce is good.

Buffet Crab

2 cups cooked rice

1 (14 ounce) can artichoke hearts, drained and halved

1 pound lump crabmeat or cooked shrimp, chopped

1/2 pound fresh mushrooms, sautéed

2 tablespoons margarine or butter

1 can cream of celery soup

1 tablespoon Worcestershire sauce

Seasoned salt to taste

1/4 cup dry white wine

3/4 cup grated sharp cheddar cheese

Combine rice, artichoke hearts, seafood and mushrooms and sauté in margarine or butter. Place in buttered 71/2"x113/4" casserole dish. Combine soup, salt, Worcestershire sauce and wine. Pour over mixture. Sprinkle grated cheese on top. Bake at 350° for 20 minutes or until bubbly. Serves 6.

Judie Grossman

Crab Soufflé

8-10 slices bread

2 cans Geisha crabmeat

1/2 cup mayonnaise (or less)

1 cup celery, chopped fine

1/2 small chopped onion

4 eggs, well beaten (or 8 egg
   whites)

3 cups milk

1 can mushroom soup,
   undiluted

1/2 cup grated sharp cheese

Pepper

Leftover can
be frozen
and reheated.

Cube 4 slices bread with crust on. Spread over
10"x14" buttered pan. Mix crabmeat, mayonnaise and
veggies (as for salad) and spoon over cubes. Quarter
remaining slices of bread with crusts removed and
place over salad mixture. Mix eggs and milk; pour
over contents and cover. Refrigerate 3 or 4 hours or
overnight. One and a half hours before serving, put in
350° oven for 15 minutes. Remove and spread warm
undiluted mushroom soup over it. Cover with cheese.
Bake in 350° for 1 hour. Serves 12.

Fran Downing

Crispy Fish Fillets

1 egg
3 tablespoons dill pickle juice
1/4 teaspoon salt
2 pounds fish fillets
1 cup or more country-style
  mashed potato flakes

Butter for frying or
combination of butter and
vegetable oil

Beat together egg, pickle juice and salt in a bowl. Dip fish in egg mixture, then in potato flakes, coating well. Fry in butter for 3-4 minutes on each side, until golden brown. Serve with lemon or cole slaw/tartar sauce. Serves 4-6.

Mickey Baumgartner

Easy Baked Scallops

1 pound fresh scallops
1/4-1/2 cup flour
Salt and pepper to taste

Fish blend herbs, if desired
Butter, to taste
1 cup Half and Half

Wash and drain scallops. Combine 1/4 to 1/2 cup flour with 1/2 teaspoon salt and a few dashes of pepper. Roll drained scallops in flour mixture (and herbs, if desired). Place scallops in greased pie plate. Dot with butter. Pour about 1 cup cream around the scallops in the baking dish, so that it will come about half way up the sides of the scallops. Bake 30-40 minutes at 350°. Serves 2-4.

Marcia Kelley

Easy Hot Weather Salmon Mousse

1 envelope Knox gelatin
2 tablespoons lemon juice
1 small onion slice, chopped
1/2 cup boiling water
1/2 cup Hellmann's mayonnaise
1/4 teaspoon paprika
1 (14 3/4 ounce) can red sockeye salmon
1 (7 1/2 ounce) can red sockeye salmon
1 teaspoon salt
1 double dash of Tabasco
1 teaspoon dried dill weed
1 cup plain yogurt
Boston lettuce (bed)

As a luncheon dish serve with crunchy pea salad (in salad section).

Add gelatin, lemon juice and onion into blender and blend on top speed with boiling water until mush. Drain and remove large salmon bones. Add deboned salmon to blender with everything else except yogurt and blend on puree until completely mixed. Add yogurt and blend thoroughly. Pour into 9"x11" glass mold, then chill. Can be made previous afternoon. Serve on Boston lettuce in scoops (like ice cream). Serves 6-8.

Maggie Foskett

El Greco's Shrimp

May be prepared up to 6-8 hours in advance; store covered in refrigerator. Reheat sauce and add shrimp just before serving.

1/2 cup minced onion

1 1/2 tablespoons butter

1 1/2 tablespoons olive oil

4 medium ripe tomatoes, peeled, seeded and chopped

1/2 cup dry white wine

1 small clove garlic, minced

1 teaspoon salt

3/4 teaspoon oregano

1/4 teaspoon freshly ground pepper

4 ounces feta cheese, crumbled

1 pound large shrimp, peeled and deveined

1/4 cup chopped fresh parsley

Sauté onion in a mixture of butter and olive oil in skillet until tender. Stir in tomatoes, white wine, garlic, salt, oregano and pepper. Bring to a boil; reduce heat. Simmer until slightly thickened, stirring constantly. Stir in cheese. Simmer for 10-15 minutes longer or until desired consistency, stirring frequently. Adjust the seasonings. Add shrimp and mix well. Cook for 5 minutes or until the shrimp turns pink, stirring frequently. Do not overcook. Spoon into bowls. Sprinkle with parsley. Serve immediately with crusty French bread. Serves 4.

Anastasia Boucoureas

Elegant Poached Salmon

Pam cooking spray or butter
3 pounds salmon fillets, skinned
1/2 cup marsala wine
2 tablespoons capers

1 bunch fresh dill or 2
  tablespoons dried dill
Knorr packaged Bernaise sauce

Line 13"x9" pan with foil. Spray foil with cooking spray. Cut salmon into 4 ounce serving pieces. Place in dish on foil. Pour wine over salmon and sprinkle with capers and dill. Cover with foil and bake at 375° for 25 minutes. Make Bernaise sauce as directed on package. Serve salmon with sauce. Garnish with extra fresh dill. Serves 12.

Jini Horan

Fillet of Sole Rive Gauche

4 fillets of sole
1/4 cup flour
Salt and pepper
1/2 cup butter, melted
1 medium onion, diced

1/2 pound fresh mushrooms,
  sliced
1 tablespoon lemon juice
1 tablespoon chopped parsley

Coat the fillets with flour, seasoned with salt and pepper to taste. Melt first 1/4-cup butter in pan and sauté filets for 2 minutes per side or until golden brown. Remove filets from pan and keep warm in oven. Melt second 1/4-cup butter and sauté the onion until transparent. Add mushrooms and cook for 2 minutes or until soft. Stir in lemon juice and parsley, seasoned with salt and pepper to taste. Pour sauce over fish and serve. Serves 4.

Frances Landau

Florida Shrimp with Pasta & Feta

A wonderful dish for buffets and barbecues-delicious served hot or at room temperature. Mixing spinach and regular linguine makes a "colorful" presentation.

2 pounds large shrimp, butterflied
1/2 pound butter
1 tablespoon olive oil
8 chopped scallions
1 pound spinach linguine
1 bunch chopped fresh basil
8-16 ounces crumbled feta cheese, to taste
Freshly ground black pepper
Cherry tomatoes, halved, for garnish

Sauté shrimp in butter and olive oil. Add and sauté the scallions. Cook and drain pasta. While hot, toss pasta with shrimp mixture, ground pepper, fresh basil and crumbled feta cheese, according to taste. Toss until cheese melts and mixture is creamy. Serve on a large platter. Garnish with cherry tomatoes. Serves 10-12.

Beverly McGeary

Fresh Salmon in Vinaigrette

1 pound salmon steaks, cut
  3/4-inch thick

Vinaigrette:
1 medium onion, chopped
1/4 teaspoon salt

1/4 teaspoon sugar
Pepper
1 bay leaf
2 cups vinegar
4 cups water

Can be made ahead of time; works well with spinach salad.

Combine all ingredients except salmon steaks in saucepan and cook rapidly for 25 minutes. Chill overnight in refrigerator. Heat oven to 325°. Pour some of boiled liquid into bottom of casserole that is large enough for salmon steaks to be placed flat. Lay salmon steaks gently in the liquid and pour remaining liquid over pieces of salmon. Bake uncovered for 25 minutes. Remove from oven and cool. Cover and refrigerate. Serving tips: Remove the steaks using a spatula. Serve with parsley mayonnaise. Serves 4.

Hella Mears Hueg

Grilled Fillet of Salmon

Use a whole salmon fillet and double the sauce for a buffet dinner.

1 stick (1/2 cup) unsalted butter

1/3 cup honey

1/3 cup brown sugar

2 tablespoons fresh lemon juice

1 teaspoon liquid smoke flavoring

1 teaspoon crushed dried red pepper flakes

1 salmon fillet, center cut, skin on and boned

Combine first 6 ingredients and cook over medium heat for 8 minutes. Cool to room temperature. Arrange salmon in dish large enough to hold it. Pour cooled marinade over salmon. Let stand for 30 minutes to an hour, refrigerated. Oil grill well and cook salmon, skin side down with lid closed for 15 to 20 minutes. Cook over medium heat. On a Weber grill set to medium-off-medium. Serve hot or at room temperature. Serves 4-6.

Gayle Gordon Nering

Grilled Swordfish

2 slices swordfish steaks

Marinade:

1/3 cup soy sauce

2 teaspoons lime zest

1/4 cup lime juice

2 garlic cloves, smashed

1 tablespoon Dijon mustard

1/4 cup peanut oil

1/4 cup chopped scallions

1/2 teaspoon salt and pepper

Trim off swordfish skin. Mix other ingredients and apply. Do not marinate longer than 1 hour. (Too long and the fish will get mushy.) Grill the fish on the "barbie" over moderate heat. Be careful not to dry out. Only takes a few minutes to cook. Serves 4.

Bob Small

Grouper Au Gratin

1/2 pound chopped mushrooms
1 cup chopped onions
1/3 cup minced parsley
1 cup dry bread crumbs
2 pounds grouper fillets
2 teaspoons salt
1 teaspoon white pepper
1/3 cup clam juice
1 cup dry white wine
1/2 cup Parmesan cheese, grated

Combine mushrooms, onions and parsley. Spread 1/2 mixture in a greased 9"x13" baking dish. Sprinkle with 1/2 cup bread crumbs. Arrange fish on top. Season with salt and pepper. Cover with rest of vegetable mixture. Pour on clam juice and wine. Bake 10 minutes at 375°. Mix cheese with remaining bread crumbs. Sprinkle over fish and vegetables. Bake 14 minutes longer until fish flakes. Serves 8.

Beth George

Grouper Tropicale

2 pounds grouper fillet
1 cup orange juice
1 or 2 ripe bananas
3 tablespoons brown sugar
Knorr Bernaise Sauce

Place grouper in a glass baking dish. Pour orange juice over the fish. Slice banana in 1/4-inch pieces and place on top of fish in a single layer. Crumble brown sugar over the top. Preheat oven to 350° and bake for 25-30 minutes until flakey. Prepare Bernaise sauce at last minute. Serve on the side of the fish.

Judy Bricker

Nicely accompanied by wild rice and steamed asparagus.

Lobster Thermidor

2 (11/2 to 2 pound) lobsters, boiled
1/4 cup butter
1/2 teaspoon paprika
1/2 cup sherry
2 tablespoons flour
2 egg yolks
2 cups Half and Half
11/2 cups sliced mushrooms, sautéed
1/2 cup grated cheese

Split lobsters lengthwise; remove all meat. Clean shell and wash well. Cut meat in large pieces. Melt butter in saucepan; add paprika, sherry and lobster. Cook for 2 minutes; fold in flour. Add egg yolks to cream; beat. Add to lobster mixture. Add 1 cup mushrooms. Cook over low heat, folding constantly until well blended and smooth. Fill shells; top with remaining mushrooms and cheese. Broil until brown. Serves 4-6.

Marcia Kelley

Lu's Scallop Castine

2 pounds large scallops, cut into bite-size pieces
1 stack Ritz crackers, buttered and crumbled
1 cup evaporated milk
1/4 cup sherry
Salt and pepper

Arrange scallops in greased baking dish–no deeper than 1/2 inch. Sprinkle half the crumbs over and then sprinkle with salt and pepper. Work crumbs into scallops. Pour milk and wine over to top. Top with remaining cracker crumbs. Bake at 350° for 1/2 hour. Serves 6.

Kay Wing

Maine Lobster Newburg

2 cups diced boiled Maine
  lobster
4 tablespoons melted butter
1 tablespoon flour
1 cup light cream

2 egg yolks, beaten
1/4 teaspoon salt
1 teaspoon lemon juice
Paprika

Heat lobster in 3 teaspoonfuls melted butter; do
not brown. Stir flour into remaining butter in another
saucepan. Add cream and heat. Stir well until smooth.
Remove from heat when mixture begins to boil. Add
egg yolks; stir until thickened. Add heated lobster, salt
and lemon juice; do not heat. Serve in patty shells or
over toast points. Sprinkle with paprika. Serves 6.

Marcia Kelley

Marinated Scallops

1/3 cup soy sauce
1/4 cup wine vinegar
2 tablespoons sugar
1 teaspoon ground ginger

1 clove garlic, pressed
1 teaspoon grated lime peel
2 pounds scallops

Combine all ingredients except scallops, mixing
well. Place scallops in an 8-inch square baking dish.
Pour marinade over scallops. Refrigerate at least 1
hour, spooning marinade over scallops frequently.
Bake at 400° for 10 minutes. Serves 8.

Judie Grossman

Maryland Lady
Crab Cakes

1 pound lump crabmeat
1/2 cup Italian seasoned
  bread crumbs
1 large egg
1/4 cup mayonnaise
1/4 teaspoon salt

1/4 teaspoon pepper
1 teaspoon Worcestershire
  sauce
1 teaspoon dry mustard
Butter or oil for frying

In a bowl, mix bread crumbs, egg, mayonnaise and seasonings. Add crabmeat and mix gently but thoroughly. If mixture is too dry, add a little more mayonnaise. Shape into 6 crab cakes. Sauté crab cakes in fry pan in just enough fat to prevent sticking, until browned; about 5 minutes on each side. If desired, crab cakes may be deep-fried at 350° for 2-3 minutes or until browned. Makes 6 crab cakes.

Nancy Porter

Orange & Bourbon Salmon

4 salmon fillets

Sauce:
1/4 cup bourbon
1/4 cup orange juice
1/4 cup soy sauce

1/4 cup brown sugar
1/4 cup chopped green onion
3 tablespoons chopped chives
2 tablespoons lemon juice
2 garlic cloves, minced

Pour sauce in bottom of baking dish. Place fish (cut into portions) skin side up in dish. Cut out wax paper in size of baking dish and fit down on top of fish. Bake 350° for 30 minutes or until fish flakes. Serves 4.

Carole Triplett

Sauce can be made in advance and stored in refrigerator for several days.

Parmesan Catfish

1/2 cup butter
1/2 teaspoon Worcestershire
   sauce
2 tablespoon lemon juice
Dash of Tabasco

Salt and pepper
1/3 cup Parmesan cheese
5 or 6 small catfish fillets,
   (3-5 ounces each)
Toasted sliced almonds

Rinse fish and drain on paper towels. Add salt and pepper to fish. Sprinkle with Parmesan cheese. Make sauce using first 5 ingredients. Pour over fish. Sprinkle with remaining Parmesan cheese. Bake fat side down at 375° for 25-30 minutes. Sprinkle with toasted almonds last 5 minutes. Bake in 2-quart Pyrex baking pan. Arrange in 1 layer. May also use individual baking dishes. Serves 3-4.

Mrs. James C. Robertson

Parmesan Sole

May use firm-fleshed fish.

4 sole fillets

3 tablespoons mayonnaise

2 tablespoons chopped scallions
or chives

1/2 cup grated Parmesan
cheese

2 tablespoons melted butter

1 dash of Tabasco sauce

1 dash lemon juice

Broil fish 4-8 minutes depending on thickness.
Combine other ingredients. Mix well and remove fish
from oven and spread mixture over top of fish.
Spread to edges. Broil 2 minutes until cheese bubbles
and browns. Watch closely to prevent burning. Serve
with sliced lemon, watercress, or parsley. Serves 4.

Isabelle Staffeldt

Roast Salmon with Asparagus

1 pound medium to thick asparagus

3 tablespoons extra virgin olive oil

Salt and freshly ground pepper

11/4 pounds (1-inch thick) salmon, (tail section)

1 tablespoon fresh lemon juice

1 teaspoon ground coriander

1/2 teaspoon dried thyme

Lemon wedges for garnish

Rinse asparagus and cut off rough ends, 4-41/2 inches. Place in large shallow 15"x10" baking dish making 1 or 2 layers. Sprinkle evenly with 1 tablespoon of olive oil; salt and pepper to taste. Toss to evenly coat. Place fish in separate baking dish. Rub with lemon juice and remaining 2 teaspoons of olive oil. Sprinkle with coriander and thyme. Lightly rub in spices. Sprinkle evenly with salt and pepper. Place both pans in oven. Bake uncovered at 450°. In 12 to 14 minutes, spears should be tender, yet crisp. Salmon should flake and have changed color in thickest part. Garnish with lemon squares. Serves 4.

Mary Helen Wyckoff

Salmon en Croute

1 pound package puff pastry	1 tablespoon butter or
1 pound salmon	margarine
1 cup white wine	Salt and pepper
8 ounces fresh mushrooms,	8 ounces Brie
sliced	1 egg white

Thaw puff pastry. Poach salmon in 1 cup wine until flaky. Sauté mushrooms in butter or margarine. Cut each sheet of pastry in half and roll out. Put 1/2 of salmon in the center of each sheet; add salt and pepper to taste. Top each with 1/2 of the mushrooms and 1/2 of the cheese. Wrap up packages and brush with egg white. Bake at 425° for 20 minutes. Serves 4.

Kay Wing

Salmon Florentine

Easy microwave dish.

1 (10 ounce) bag fresh	Lemon slices
spinach	Salt and pepper to taste
2 (8 ounce) salmon steaks	

Place spinach in microwave casserole using casserole that best fits the salmon. Cover. Microwave on high 3 minutes. Place salmon on spinach, skin side up. Cover and microwave for 5 minutes. Remove skin and cover with lemon slices. Remove to plates so that spinach remains under the salmon. Serve with lemon wedges on the side. Serves 2.

Patricia Bush

Scalloped Oysters

1 stick butter

30 saltine crackers

1 pint oysters, drained (save liquid)

Salt and pepper

3 tablespoons oyster liquid

3 tablespoons cream

Melt butter and mix in cracker crumbs made from saltine crackers. Butter 2-quart oval or oblong casserole. Preheat oven to 400°. Divide crumbs into thirds. Layer oysters and crackers starting with cracker crumbs, then oysters. Add salt and pepper, 1/2 oyster liquid, and 1/2 cream. Repeat, ending with top layer of crumbs, never more than 2 layers of oysters. Bake 30 minutes at 400°. Serves 4.

Elizabeth Perkins

Scallops with Grand Marnier

1 pound scallops	1/4 cup Grand Marnier
3 tablespoons unsalted butter	1 cup heavy cream
1/2 cup minced shallots	1 teaspoon grated orange rind
11/2 cup chicken broth	Salt and pepper
1/2 cup dry white wine	Lemon juice
1/2 cup orange juice	

In large skillet cook scallops seasoned with salt and pepper in 11/2 tablespoons butter for 1 minute, stirring. Cover and cook scallops 2 minutes more. Stir occasionally until opaque and just firm. Transfer scallops with slotted spoon to large warm plate. Add shallots to skillet and cook for 1 minute. Add broth, wine, juice and Grand Marnier and boil to reduce to 2/3 cup. Add cream and simmer until lightly thickened. Whisk in remaining butter and rind and season with lemon juice. Pour over scallops and serve. Nice to serve in coquille shell dishes. Serves 4.

Joann Duncan

Sebastian's Scallops Oregano

1 pound scallops, drained and
patted dry

1/2 teaspoon salt

1/8 teaspoon pepper

2 cups Italian-style
bread crumbs

2 large lemons (one juiced
and one grated or zest)

2 tablespoons paprika

2 ounces cooking sherry wine

1/4 teaspoon oregano

4 tablespoons butter

Wash scallops, drain and pat dry. Cut into uniform sizes. Combine all dry ingredients. Add sherry wine, juice of 1 lemon and butter. "Fluff" mixture together. Roll scallops in bread crumbs. Place in lightly buttered 8"x8" casserole dish. Cover top of casserole with bread crumbs. Bake at 350° for 20 minutes or until scallops are golden brown. "Dash" with sherry wine and sprinkle with grated lemon rind or lemon zest. Serves 4.

Sebastian Paguni

Shrimp & Cheese Soufflé

6 slices bread
1/2 pound Colby cheese, sliced
1 pound cooked shrimp
1/4 cup butter, melted

3 whole eggs, beaten
1/2 teaspoon dry mustard
Pinch of salt
1 pint milk

Remove crusts from bread and break bread into pieces the size of a quarter. Break cheese into bite-size pieces. Arrange bread, then cheese and then shrimp into 2 layers in a greased 2 or 3-quart casserole. Pour melted butter over the mixture. Beat eggs; add mustard and salt to eggs; then add milk and mix all. Pour over dry ingredients in casserole. Let stand covered at least 3 hours (preferably overnight). Bake at 350° for 1 hour. Serves 6.

Jean Sampson

Shrimp Curry with Egg Noodles

1 can cream of shrimp soup
1 cup sour cream
1/2 stick butter
1 level tablespoon curry
powder

1 pound cooked shrimp
16 ounces egg noodles

Mix all ingredients together except shrimp and noodles. Heat in casserole dish in oven at 325° until mixture is bubbly (not boiling). Fold in shrimp and heat until shrimp are hot, approximately 8 minutes. Serve over cooked noodles.

Mary Helen Wyckoff

Shrimp & Feta Cheese over Angel Hair Pasta

3 cloves garlic, minced

1 medium onion, chopped

3 small yellow-green peppers, in rings

1 tablespoon butter

1 tablespoon olive oil

2 tablespoons red wine

2 plum tomatoes, chopped

2 green onions, sliced (include green)

1 pound raw peeled shrimp

1 tablespoon olive oil

1/4 pound crumbled feta cheese

6 ounces angel hair pasta

You need one large sauté pan and one medium sauté pan for cooking the shrimp.

Sauté the first 6 ingredients in a large or medium size sauté pan. Cook for 5 minutes. Add the plum tomatoes and onion; cook 2 more minutes. Meanwhile, cook pasta according to package. In separate pan cook the shrimp in 1 tablespoon oil for about 2-3 minutes. Pour into first pan. Mix together. Heat together for 3 minutes. Top with crumbled feta. Let set for 5 minutes. Serve over cooked pasta. Serves 2.

Joan Murray

Shrimp de Jonghe

2 pounds uncooked shrimp,
  shelled and deveined
1/3 cup vegetable oil
1/2 cup flaked coconut
1/4 cup dried bread crumbs
  (fine)

3 tablespoons chopped parsley
2-3 cloves minced garlic
Salt and freshly ground pepper
1/4 teaspoon paprika
Dash cayenne or Tabasco
1/4 cup sherry

Combine ingredients except shrimp and sherry, reserving 1/4 cup for topping. Toss shrimp to coat. Turn into 11/2 quart casserole. Pour sherry over. Sprinkle with reserved mixture. Bake uncovered in 375° oven until shrimp are tender, about 20 minutes. Serves 4-6.

Roberta Tharpe

Shrimp & Sun-Dried Tomatoes with Linguine

1/2 pound linguine

2 tablespoons unsalted butter

2 tablespoons olive oil

1/2 cup coarsely chopped onion

2 cloves garlic, minced

1/4 cup sun-dried tomatoes, in oil, drained and cut into strips

1/4 cup minced parsley

1 tablespoon capers

1/2 cup dry white wine

12 jumbo shrimp, peeled and deveined

2 tablespoons Dijon mustard

1/2 cup heavy cream

Salt and pepper to taste

Tarragon sprigs to garnish

Cook linguine while preparing recipe. Heat butter and oil in heavy skillet over medium heat. Add onion, garlic, tomatoes, parsley and capers. Sauté over medium heat until onions are translucent. Add wine and simmer for 2 minutes. Add shrimp, cook until pink, about 2 minutes. Add mustard and cream and stir about 2 minutes. Season with salt and pepper. Serve shrimp over linguine garnished with tarragon. Serves 2.

Lynne Clark Nordhoff

South Carolina Shrimp Creole

11/2 pound cooked shrimp
12 slices bacon
2 bell peppers, chopped
1/2 medium onion, chopped
3 sticks celery, chopped
1 large can tomato juice

1 stick butter or margarine
Salt and pepper, to taste
2 cups cooked rice
1 teaspoon sugar
11/2 teaspoons sage

Fry bacon until crisp. Drain, reserving 3 tablespoons fat, then crumble. Sauté next 3 ingredients in fat. Add tomato juice, sugar, sage and simmer 5 minutes. Add margarine, salt and pepper and rice. Simmer 11/2- 2 hours. Add shrimp last 15 minutes before serving. Serves 6-8.

Irma Dralle-Meyer

Spicy Baked Shrimp

1/4 cup olive oil
1/4 cup white wine
2 tablespoons cajun seasoning
2 tablespoons lemon juice
2 tablespoons chopped fresh parsley

1 tablespoon honey
2 tablespoon soy sauce
1-2 cloves garlic, crushed
11/2 pounds raw shrimp, shelled

Combine all ingredients except the shrimp. Place shrimp in a 9"x13" baking dish. When ready to bake, pour sauce over shrimp. Bake at 450°, uncovered for 10-12 minutes. Serve with lemon wedges and french bread or over rice or thin pasta. Serves 4-6.

Delores Gaeta

Spicy Sautéed Fish with Olives & Cherry Tomatoes

1/4 cup light olive oil

2 pounds tilapia, red snapper or orange roughy

1/2 cup chopped fresh parsley

1/2 teaspoon dried, crushed red pepper flakes

4 cups cherry tomatoes, halved

1 cup kalamata olives, chopped

6 garlic cloves, peeled

Salt and pepper

Heat oil in heavy skillet over medium heat. Sprinkle fish with salt and pepper. Sauté fish until just opaque in center (3 minutes per side). Transfer fish to platter; keep warm. Add parsley and red pepper flakes to same skillet. Sauté for 1 minute. Add tomatoes, olives and garlic. Sauté until tomatoes are soft and juicy, about 2 minutes. Season sauce with salt and pepper. Spoon over fish. Serves 6.

Sally Lopez

Szechwan Shrimp

2 tablespoons oil
1 pound large raw shrimp, peeled
2 tablespoons minced fresh ginger
3 garlic cloves, minced
2 tablespoons sherry
2 tablespoons soy sauce
4 tablespoons ketchup
4 tablespoons chili sauce
1 teaspoon hot red pepper flakes
1/4 pound chopped green onion
1 pound linguine, cooked
1/2-3/4 pound snow peas

Heat oil in wok or skillet, while also preparing linguine and snow peas separately. Add shrimp, onion, ginger and garlic. Stir-fry until shrimp are pink. Blend in sherry and soy sauce. Add remaining ingredients and stir well. Serve with linguini and steamed snow peas. Serves 4.

Lynda Bulloch

Tropical Lemon Sole

2 servings lemon sole fillets
Seasoned bread crumbs
1 tablespoon butter
1 tablespoon fresh or dried chopped parsley
1 garlic clove, cut in half
1 cup orange juice
Juice from 1/2 fresh lemon
1 cup dry white wine
Lemon wedges
Olive oil

Preheat oven to 350°. Coat shallow casserole dish or baking pan with olive oil. Arrange fish fillets; sprinkle with bread crumbs. Add butter, parsley, garlic, orange juice and lemon juice. Bake 12-15 minutes. Add 1 cup white wine. Bake 5 minutes. Serve fish filets with pan juices, lemon wedges and steamed broccoli or vegetable of choice. Serves 2.

Suzanne Chute

The Art of Cooking • Seafood

Poultry

Almond Chicken Avocado
Apricot Chicken
Baked French Chicken
Bourbon Chicken
Canard à la Christophe with Cherry & Fig Sauce
Chicken Breast Supreme
Chicken Casserole
Chicken Chili
Chicken Curry
Chicken Delicious
Chicken Imperial
Chicken à Madras
Chicken Mandoo
Chicken with Orange-Mango Sauce
Chicken-Rice Casserole
Chicken Supreme
Concert Casserole
Curried Chicken
Florentine Chicken
Goldies' Chicken
Joan's Quick & Easy Baked Chicken Casserole
Lemon Chicken Scallopini
Mozart's Chicken Piccata
Orange Cornish Hens with Apricots
Peachy Chicken
Rock Cornish Game Hens with Wild Rice Dressing
Rolled Stuffed Chicken Breasts
Skillet Turkey with Bows
Tanger Chicken
Tarragon Chicken
Turkey Crème Supreme
Turkey & Rice Casserole
Turkey Tetrazinni
White Chicken Lasagna

Almond Chicken Avocado

5 pounds chicken breasts

1 pound mushrooms

1 can cream of chicken soup

1/2 teaspoon salt

1/2 cup grated cheddar cheese

1/2 cup dry sherry

Pinch of rosemary

Pinch of basil

Dash of Tabasco

2 ripe avocados, sliced

1/2 cup toasted slivered almonds

Simmer breasts for 20 minutes. Take meat from bones and cut into bite-size slivers. Sprinkle with salt. Wash mushrooms, slice and cook in butter until tender, then sprinkle with salt. Combine soup, sherry, cheese and seasonings. Arrange chicken and mushrooms in 3-quart casserole. Pour over soup mixture. Cover and bake at 350° for 25 minutes. Uncover and add avocados. Bake uncovered for 10 minutes. Sprinkle with almonds. Serves 8-10.

Joanne Bodine

When toasting almonds-watch carefully—they burn easily.

Apricot Chicken

Good served
cold.

8 boneless, skinless chicken
  breasts
1 head of garlic, peeled and
  chopped
3 tablespoons herbs de
  Provence
Salt to taste

1 cup dried apricots
1 cup pitted green olives
1 1/2 cups dry white wine
1/2 cup capers
1 cup brown sugar
1/2 cup olive oil
Chopped parsley

Marinate chicken with garlic, herbs, salt, 1/2 cup wine, apricots, olives and capers. Cover and refrigerate overnight. Preheat oven to 350°. Arrange chicken in a single layer in jellyroll pan. Cover with marinade and sprinkle with brown sugar. Pour over 1 cup wine and olive oil. Bake for 45 minutes, until cooked through, basting frequently. Remove to serving dish and garnish with parsley. Serves 8-12.

Sally Wiley

Baked French Chicken

1/4 cup butter
1 broiler fryer or chicken breast
1 medium onion, chopped
1/2 pound mushrooms, sliced
1 can cream of mushroom soup

3/4 cup sherry or white wine
1 tablespoon chopped parsley
1 teaspoon salt
1 teaspoon paprika
1-2 lemon slices
1/2 cup pimento olives, sliced
Grind of fresh pepper

Melt butter in large skillet over medium heat. Add chicken pieces or breasts equivalent to 1 chicken and brown slowly on both sides. Remove from skillet and place in shallow baking dish. Add onion and mushrooms to butter in skillet and cook until limp. Stir pepper, paprika, soup, sherry, parsley, olives, salt and lemon slices. Pour over chicken in casserole. Bake 1 hour at 350° until tender. May serve with noodles or rice. Serves 4.

Irma Dralle-Meyer

Bourbon Chicken

Can be put together in morning and baked at night.

8 chicken breasts, boned and halved
Flour
Salt and pepper
Paprika
1/2 cup butter
1 pound fresh mushrooms, sliced

2 (10 ounce) cans cream of chicken soup
2 ounces bourbon
3/4 teaspoon curry powder
Parsley
Slivered almonds

Dust chicken with flour, salt, pepper and paprika. Sauté in hot butter until brown. Place in 11"x13" casserole dish. In same butter, sauté mushrooms and add to chicken. Add bourbon, undiluted soup and curry powder to skillet. Stir to make a smooth thick sauce. Pour over chicken and mushrooms. Sprinkle with parsley and almonds. Bake at 350° for 1 hour. Serves 8-10.

Sally Taylor

Canard á la Christophe with Cherry & Fig Sauce

3 ready to cook ducks, 4 pounds each

2 teaspoons salt

3 small onions, peeled and quartered

1 large apple, cored and sliced

Cherry and Fig Sauce:

2 tablespoons cornstarch

1/4 teaspoon salt

1/4 teaspoon powdered mustard

1 cup water

1/4 cup thawed orange juice concentrate

1 (13 ounce) can whole figs

1 (14 ounce) can dark sweet cherries, pitted

2 tablespoons butter

1 tablespoon soy sauce

If canned figs are not available, table figs may be used. Bring to boil in saucepan with water and simmer until puffed. Quarter each fig after removing stems. This dish may be made ahead of time. Reheat before serving.

Preheat oven to 325°. Wash ducks in cold water and dry. Discard giblets and excess fat from body cavities. Rub salt in the cavities and over the skins. Put 1 onion and 1/3 of the apple slices in the cavity of each duck. Close openings with skewers. Place ducks, breast up, on rack in a shallow roasting pan. Roast, uncovered, 2 1/2 hours until ducks are tender, brown and crisp. Pierce skins frequently with the tines of a fork. Cut ducks in quarters and place them on a very large warmed platter. Sauce: In a 1 1/2-quart saucepan, mix cornstarch, salt and mustard. Add water and orange juice and mix well. Drain syrup from figs and cherries, each in a separate bowl. Measure 1/4 cup of the fig syrup and 2 tablespoons of the cherry juice and add to cornstarch mixture. Bring the mixture to boiling point, over moderate heat, stirring constantly. Boil for 3 minutes. Add drained figs, cherries, butter and soy sauce. Heat only until sauce bubbles. Serve with roast duck. Spoon some of the cherry and fig sauce over the ducks. Serves 8-12.

Tannis Richardson

Chicken Breast Supreme

2 pounds chicken breast
Flour
1/4 cup butter
1/2 pound sliced boiled ham
1 pound sliced mushrooms
16-20 tiny potatoes (canned are OK)
2 tablespoons tarragon vinegar
2 tablespoons sauterne wine
1/2 tablespoon paprika
1/8 teaspoon cayenne
1 tablespoon sugar
1 clove garlic, pressed
1/4 cup salad oil
Salt and pepper to taste

Roll chicken in flour and sauté over moderate heat in butter. Mix last 7 ingredients (plus salt and pepper) and pour over chicken. Baste often for 20 minutes. Brown potatoes and mushrooms in butter. Place ham in casserole. Place chicken on top and potatoes and mushrooms over all. Pour sauce and butter over dish. Cover and bake in a 7"x11" flat-bottomed Pyrex dish for 45 minutes in 350° oven. Baste often. Serves 6.

Fairfield Frank Dubois

Chicken Casserole

2 cups cooked chicken

1 can Healthy Request mushroom soup

1 can Healthy Request cream of chicken soup

1 small can Chinese noodles

1 can water chestnuts, sliced and drained

1/4 cup milk

1/4 cup salad dressing (Hellmann's)

1 1/2 teaspoons Worcestershire sauce

Crushed potato chips

Delicious, simple dish.

Mix all ingredients together and top with crushed potato chips. Put into 9"x13" dish and bake at 350° for 45 minutes. Serves 8-10.

Joan Buehler

Chicken Chili

3 medium boneless chicken breasts

1 medium onion, diced

2 tablespoons salad oil

3 tablespoons chili powder

2 (16 ounce) cans chunky tomatoes

1 (16 ounce) can whole kernel corn, drained

1 (15-19 ounce) can red kidney beans

1 tablespoon chopped jalapeño pepper (optional)

Cut chicken into 1/2-inch chunks. Cook onion in hot salad oil for 5 minutes. Add chicken and brown lightly. Stir in chili powder and cook 1 minute. Add remaining ingredients and heat on high until boiling. Reduce heat to low, cover and simmer for 30 minutes. Serve in a bowl or in tortilla cups with chopped fresh tomatoes and shredded lettuce. Serves 6.

Billie Stevens

Chicken Curry

4 chicken breasts

2 cans cream of chicken soup

1 1/2 cups mayonnaise

2 teaspoons lemon juice

1 teaspoon curry powder

2/3 cup sharp cheddar cheese

3/4 cup bread cubes

2 tablespoons butter

Boil and split chicken breasts. Make sauce of soup, mayonnaise, lemon juice and curry powder. Pour over cooked, deboned chicken. Pack in bottom of 8"x10" baking dish. Top with shredded cheese and bread cubes cooked in butter. Bake at 350° for 1 hour-1 hour 15 minutes. Serves 6.

Virginia Quirk

Chicken Delicious

5 chicken breasts (cooked, boned and cubed)

1 (81/2 ounce) can water chestnuts, sliced

1/2 pound sliced mushrooms, sautéed

1 1/2 cups finely chopped celery

1 can cream of mushroom soup

1 cup mayonnaise

2 cups Pepperidge Farm cornbread stuffing mix

1/2 cup melted butter

Grease 12"x8"x2" baking dish. Mix water chestnuts, mushrooms, celery, soup and mayonnaise. Place chicken in dish. Pour soup mix over chicken ("frost" the chicken with it as the mix is thick). Mix the stuffing with melted butter and spread over top of casserole. Bake for 45 minutes at 350°. Serves: 8-10.

Joyce Vitelli

Chicken Imperial

6 boneless chicken breasts
1 teaspoon salt
2 teaspoons Worcestershire
   sauce
1 teaspoon curry powder
1 teaspoon oregano

3/4 cup margarine, melted
1/2 teaspoon dry mustard
1/2 teaspoon garlic powder
1/4 teaspoon paprika
2-3 dashes Tabasco
1/2 cup dry sherry

Garnish with spiced peaches and parsley. Serve with rice.

Season chicken on both sides with salt. Place breast in shallow pan. Blend remaining ingredients and brush generously with sauce. Bake in moderate oven at 325°, turning and basting breasts with sauce. Bake about 1 hour (less for smaller breasts). Serve on warm platter. Serves 4-6.

Joan Dunham

Chicken á Madras

4 small chicken breasts or 8
   tenders
Flour
4 tablespoons butter
1/2 cup chopped yellow onions
4 cloves of garlic

1 tablespoon ginger root, grated
2 teaspoons curry powder
1 cup chicken broth
2 tablespoons mango chutney
3/4 cup heavy cream

Dust chicken breasts in flour, sauté in butter and set aside in warm oven. Sauté onions in butter for 4 minutes, add garlic and sauté for 2 more minutes. Add gingerroot, curry powder, chicken broth and mango chutney. Reduce volume to 1/2. Add heavy cream and cook 4-5 minutes more to finish the sauce. Add chicken to sauce to warm and serve over rice (basmati). Garnish with cilantro. Serves 4.

Isabelle Staffeldt

Chicken Mandoo

Use any parts of the chicken, but boneless thighs are the best. Sauce also good to put on the rice.

1 can cranberry sauce (whole or jellied)

1/2 bottle Catalina dressing

1 package onion soup mix

8-10 chicken parts

Mix first 3 ingredients together; pour over chicken. Place all the ingredients in a 12"x13" baking pan. Bake at 250° for 1 hour and at 350° for 1/2 hour-1 hour. Serve with rice. Serves 4-6.

Mary Elizabeth Smith

Chicken with Orange-Mango Sauce

2 tablespoons butter or olive oil

4 chicken breast halves

Salt, pepper and garlic salt

1 cup orange juice

1 tablespoon orange marmalade

1 ripe mango, mashed or diced

1 red pepper, sliced

1 whole jalapeño, chopped

Season chicken breast halves with salt, pepper and garlic salt. Sauté in butter or olive oil until nicely browned. Add remaining ingredients and cook until chicken breasts are no longer pink and sauce has thickened. Mango will thicken sauce. Serve with white or brown rice. Serves 4.

Ruth Gusdorf

Chicken-Rice Casserole

4 cups chicken breast, cooked and cubed

1 box Uncle Ben's Original Long Grain & Wild Rice

1 can French green beans, drained

1 can sliced water chestnuts, drained

1 can cream of celery soup

1 small jar pimientos

1 cup mayonnaise

1/2 cup fresh sliced mushrooms

1/2 cup chopped onion

1/4 cup butter

Salt and pepper to taste

2 cups sharp cheddar cheese

Cook rice as per directions; add chicken. Mix with green beans, water chestnuts, celery soup, pimientos and mayonnaise. Sauté mushrooms and onions in butter or margarine and mix with all ingredients above. Place in greased 9"x13" casserole. Top with cheese. Bake at 350° for 30 minutes or until bubbly. Let stand 10 minutes. Serves 10-12.

Mary McCarthy

Chicken Supreme

2 cups milk

1 cup cream

2 tablespoons butter (level)

2 tablespoons flour (heaping)

4 eggs, separated

4 cups flaked chicken

1/2 pound blanched almonds, coarsely chopped

1 can chow mein noodles

1 pound mushrooms, cut up

2 cups milk

1 cup cream

2 tablespoons butter

2 tablespoons flour

Make sauce of first 4 ingredients and beaten egg yolks. Combine with chicken and almonds and add beaten egg whites last. Place in buttered casserole with noodles on bottom and top and bake in moderate oven, about 30 minutes. Serve with mushroom sauce. To make: sauté mushrooms, make cream sauce and add mushrooms. Seasons to taste. Serves 12.

Pat Hartman

Concert Casserole

3 whole chicken breasts, cooked
2 (13 3/4 ounce) cans
   artichoke hearts
2 1/2 cups Hellmann's
   mayonnaise
1 small jar pimientos, finely
   chopped

1 1/4 cup freshly grated
   Parmesan cheese
1/2 pound sautéed fresh
   mushrooms
Paprika

Skin, bone and cut cooked chicken breasts in bite-size pieces. Drain artichokes and cut each into 6 pieces. Combine all ingredients, reserving 1/2 cup of cheese for top of casserole. Bake in non-greased, uncovered casserole dish at 350° for 30 minutes. Sprinkle with paprika before serving. Serves 6.

JoAnn Ward

Curried Chicken

1/4 cup all-purpose flour

2 teaspoons salt

1 teaspoon white pepper

8 chicken breast halves, skinned and boned

1/2 cup butter

3/4 cup chopped onions

2 medium green peppers, seeded and chopped

2 small garlic cloves or 1/2 teaspoon garlic powder

2 (141/2 ounce) cans tomato wedges

1 (141/2 ounce) can seasoned tomato sauce

11/2 to 2 teaspoons curry powder

1/2 cup raisins

Package slivered almonds, toasted

Chopped parsley

Cooked rice and chutney

Combine flour with 1 teaspoon salt and 1/4 teaspoon pepper in plastic bag. Shake chicken, 1 piece at a time, in flour to coat. Brown chicken in butter. Remove and keep warm. Add onion, green pepper and garlic to skillet. Sauté until soft. Add tomatoes, tomato sauce, curry powder, remaining salt and 3/4 teaspoon pepper. Simmer uncovered for 10 minutes. Place chicken in 13"x9"x2" baking dish. Add raisins and sauce. Cover and bake at 325° for 11/2 hours. Garnish with almonds and parsley. Serve with hot fluffy rice and chutney. Serves 8.

Milly Ann Stewart

Florentine Chicken

6 half breasts chicken, boned
   and skinned
Salt and pepper
1/2 stick butter
2 tablespoons oil
2 (10 ounce) packages frozen
   chopped spinach
1/2 cup Hellmann's mayonnaise

1/4 cup sour cream
1 can cream of chicken soup
1 tablespoon lemon juice
1 teaspoon curry powder
1/2 cup sharp cheddar cheese,
   grated
1/2 cup corn flake crumbs
Sliced almonds

Preheat oven to 350°. Squeeze spinach dry. Spread in bottom of greased 2-quart casserole dish. Sauté chicken lightly in butter and oil, then place on spinach. Mix mayonnaise, sour cream, chicken soup, lemon juice and curry powder. Pour over chicken. Top with grated cheese, crumbs and almonds. Bake at 350° for 1/2 hour. Serves 6.

Roberta Tharpe

Goldies' Chicken

1 cup crème fraiche
1/2 cup dry sherry
1/4 cup Dijon mustard
4 teaspoons dried tarragon

Salt and pepper to taste
8 boneless, skinless chicken
   breasts

Stir together first 5 ingredients. Coat chicken and place in a 9"x13" baking dish. Pour remaining sauce over chicken. Bake at 350°, uncovered, for 30 minutes. Serves 4.

Lynda Goldie

Joan's Quick & Easy Baked Chicken Casserole

Good way to use leftover turkey or chicken.

1/2 cup instant rice
1 small jar mushrooms, stems and pieces, drained
1 can condensed cheddar cheese soup
2 cups chicken breasts, cut in bite-size pieces

1 package frozen peas, defrosted
1/2 cup milk
1 cup water
2 cups cheese crackers, crushed

Preheat oven to 325°. Cook rice with water as directed on package. Place rice in an 8"x10" greased baking dish. Cover rice with chicken pieces. Spread mushrooms and peas over chicken. Mix canned soup with milk. Stir until smooth; pour into dish. Spread crushed crackers evenly over mixture. Cover baking dish and bake for 40 minutes. Let stand for 5 minutes before serving. Serves 4.

Joan Macarthy

Lemon Chicken Scallopini

2 pounds boneless, skinless chicken breasts, cut into 4 pieces

3/4 teaspoon salt

1/2 teaspoon freshly ground pepper

4 teaspoons cornstarch

4 tablespoons canola oil

1 egg white

1/4 cup flour

1/2 stick butter

1 whole lemon, thinly sliced

2 tablespoons fresh lemon juice

1 clove garlic

1/4 cup water

2 tablespoons parsley, chopped

I prefer using chicken breasts for scallopini instead of veal. It is more predictable—and simply delicious.

Cut chicken breasts into 4 pieces. Pound each chicken breast until sort of flat and even in shape. Put into glass dish and sprinkle with salt and pepper. Let stand 20 minutes. Fold in egg white and let stand for 30 minutes. Shake off excess egg white and coat lightly with flour. Sauté chicken over medium heat in butter for 4 minutes until opaque and golden brown on both sides. Remove to platter and keep warm. Add lemon slices to drippings. Add lemon juice, garlic and water. Cook, stirring, over high heat and reduce. Pour over chicken and sprinkle with parsley. Serves 4.

Frances Luessenhop

Mozart's Chicken Piccata

4 whole chicken breasts
1/4 cup flour
1 1/2 teaspoons salt
1/4 teaspoon freshly ground
  pepper
1/4 cup clarified butter

1 tablespoon olive oil
2-4 tablespoons dry white wine
3 tablespoons lemon juice
Lemon slices
3 tablespoons capers
1/4 cup fresh parsley, chopped

Skin, bone and cut chicken in half; pound chicken breasts thin between two sheets of wax paper. Combine flour, salt and pepper and coat chicken breasts with mixture. In large skillet, heat butter and oil. Sauté breasts until gold brown (2-3 minutes per side). Place on platter and keep warm. Stir wine into skillet and scrape bottom to loosen all drippings. Add lemon juice; blend well. Return chicken to pan and continue to cook until sauce thickens. Add lemon slices, capers and parsley. Serve immediately. Serves 8.

Nancy Porter

Orange Cornish Hens with Apricots

2 or 4 (1/4 pound) Cornish
  hens
1/4 cup orange juice
1/2 cup apricot preserves
21/2 teaspoons Dijon mustard
1/2 teaspoon rosemary

1/2 teaspoon thyme
1/4 teaspoon cayenne pepper
1 clove garlic, minced
1/4 teaspoon salt
1 can drained apricot halves

Brush hens with 1 tablespoon orange juice. Roast at 325° for 11/2-13/4 hours. Make sauce by mixing remaining ingredients (except whole apricots) and brush on hens during roasting. Mix pan juices and apricots with remaining sauce. Heat and pour over hens and rice. Serves 2-4.

Anne Lynn

Peachy Chicken

6 chicken breasts, halved,
  skinless and boneless
Flour, for dredging
Butter, for browning
1 1/2 cups orange juice
2 tablespoons vinegar, not
  white

2 tablespoons brown sugar
1 teaspoon dried basil
1/2 teaspoon nutmeg
1 can peach halves, drained

Dredge chicken in flour. Brown in butter. Place chicken in large baking dish. Mix orange juice and spices together. Pour over chicken. Cover and bake at 350° until tender, about 1 hour. Add peaches about 10 minutes prior to serving. Can be made ahead of time and frozen without the peaches. Serves 6.

Carol Conant

Rock Cornish Game Hens with Wild Rice Dressing

1 cup wild rice

21/2 cups water

1/2 can water chestnuts, chopped

1-2 (4 ounce) cans chopped mushrooms, drained

1/2-1 teaspoon sage

1 teaspoon salt; pepper to taste

2 cloves garlic, minced

1/2 medium onion, chopped

2 Cornish game hens, split, rinsed and blot dried

Sauce:

2 tablespoons olive oil

1/2 pound melted butter

Juice of 1/2-1 lemon, seeded

Place rice in cold water and bring to a boil. Lower heat and simmer uncovered until almost absorbed. Add water chestnuts and mushrooms. Add sage, salt, pepper, 1 clove garlic and onion. Mix well together and place in bottom of 9"x15"x2" baking dish for 2 small birds or 1 large bird. Baste split birds inside and out with basting sauce. Sauce: Melt butter and add olive oil, remaining clove of garlic, minced, and lemon juice. Whip to emulsify. Place basted birds, skin side up and cover with foil. Bake 1/2 hour to 45 minutes, basting frequently. For the last 10-15 minutes, uncover and baste well. Bake until browned. Serves 4.

Lynn Schneider

Rolled Stuffed Chicken Breasts

1 chicken breast butterflied and pounded to 1/2-inch thick

Small, thin slices of ham

Small, thin slices of Swiss cheese

Panko (Japanese) bread crumbs

Hot paprika

Salt

Oregano (or curry)

1 tablespoon sweet butter

2 tablespoons extra virgin olive oil

Pound breast to about 1/2-inch thick. Lay ham slice on chicken breast and then cheese flat and roll in saran wrap, making a tight roll. Refrigerate 3-4 hours or overnight. Unwrap and roll in panko bread crumbs seasoned with paprika, salt and oregano or curry. Sauté in sweet butter and olive oil mix until brown all over, about 4-5 minutes. Place in baking pan in 350° oven for 20 minutes. Remove and let sit for 10 minutes and slice about 1 inch thick. Serves 2.

Richard Koff

Skillet Turkey with Bows

3/4 pound ground turkey
1 medium onion, chopped
1/4 teaspoon garlic
  powder
1 (141/2 ounce) can stewed
  tomatoes
1/4 cup soy sauce

11/4 teaspoons dried basil,
  crumbled
11/4 cup water
21/2 cups uncooked bowtie
  macaroni
1 (9 ounces) package frozen
  Italian green beans

In large skillet with cover, cook turkey with onion
and garlic powder over medium-high heat, breaking
up large chunks. Stir in tomatoes, soy sauce, basil and
11/4 cups water; cover and bring to a boil. Stir in
macaroni; cover and return to boil. Reduce heat and
simmer for 15 minutes, stirring once. Stir in green
beans; cover and return to boil. Reduce heat and simmer 10-12 minutes or longer until macaroni and
beans are tender; stir occasionally. Serves 4.

Hildegard Murray

Tanger Chicken

3 tablespoons Chinese mustard
2 tablespoons orange
  marmalade
1/3 cup honey

1 tablespoon cumin
Juice of 1 tangerine
5 large chicken breast halves,
  with skin

Preheat oven to 400°. Combine first 5 ingredients
with fork or small whip. Place chicken skin side down
in foil-lined pan. Brush sauce over chicken. Turn over.
Push skin back and brush meat with sauce. Pull skin
back and brush with remaining sauce. Bake for 30-35
minutes until juices run clear when pricked with a
fork. Do not overcook. Serves 5.

Rochelle Kay

Tarragon Chicken

Can make ahead and freeze without baking. Defrost day of use and bake until hot and bubbly. Also good with pheasant, instead of chicken.

6 chicken breasts, cut in bite-size pieces
Paprika, salt and pepper
11/2 sticks butter
2 (15 ounce) cans artichoke hearts
1 pound fresh mushrooms, sliced
1/4 teaspoon tarragon
6 tablespoons flour
1 cup cocktail sherry
3 cups chicken bouillon
8 large kaiser rolls
Melted butter

Heat oven to 350°. Coat chicken pieces with paprika, salt and pepper. Sauté chicken in 1 stick of butter. Place in casserole and add drained artichokes. Place mushrooms and additional butter in same skillet, season with tarragon, and sauté for 5 minutes. Sprinkle in flour and add sherry and bouillon. Simmer 5 minutes and pour over chicken and artichokes. Cover casserole and bake for 45 minutes. Hollow out rolls and brush with melted butter. Heat rolls in 400° oven; serve chicken scooped into rolls. Serves 8.

Jean Beaver

Turkey Crème Supreme

3/4 cup celery, cut into 1/2-
inch pieces
1/8 pound butter
4 tablespoons flour
11/2 cups milk
1 cup chopped, diced turkey
(white and dark meat),
cooked

1/4 teaspoon salt
2 tablespoons Worcestershire
sauce
Pinch of chopped garlic with
parsley
Paprika

Cook celery in water on slow boil for 5 minutes and drain. Melt butter in 2-quart pot on simmer. Blend flour in with whisk over low heat. Slowly add milk and blend with whisk until it thickens. Add turkey and celery. Continue to slow cook and mix for 5 minutes. Blend in salt, Worcestershire and garlic to taste. Serve plain or over toast points. Sprinkle with paprika before serving. Serves 6.

Ellen & Vince Kiernan

Turkey & Rice Casserole

1 pound ground turkey
1 medium onion, chopped
1 package rice pilaf
1 tablespoon margarine

1 cup canned chicken broth
11/3 cups water
1/2 cup slivered almonds
1/2 cup golden raisins

Cook turkey in large skillet until done, stirring often. Add chopped onion, mix thoroughly, cover and simmer for 5-7 minutes. Add in margarine, chicken broth and water. Mix and bring to a boil on a higher flame. Lower heat: add almonds and raisins. Mix, cover and simmer for 25 minutes. Serves 4-6.

Mrs. Michal Wiesler

Turkey Tetrazinni

2 tablespoons margarine
2 tablespoons chopped onion
1 cup chicken broth
1 can cream of mushroom soup
2 cups cubed turkey
1 teaspoon chopped parsley
1/8 teaspoon white pepper
1 can mushrooms, drained
1 (8 ounce) package
  spaghetti, cooked

In Dutch oven, melt margarine in medium heat. Lightly brown onion, add broth, then soup. Stir until smooth. Add turkey, parsley, pepper and mushrooms. Reduce heat to low and cook 5-7 minutes, stirring occasionally. Drop in spaghetti; stir and heat thoroughly. Serves 4.

Mae Castello

White Chicken Lasagna

Total cheese will be 6 cups—4 cups for chicken mixture and 2 cups for layering. Use lasagna noodles that do not need to be pre-cooked. So easy!

6 boneless chicken breasts, cubed
6 green onions, sliced to include green top
2 cans green chiles, mild and chopped
1 can cream of chicken soup
1/2 cup sour cream
6 cups shredded Monterey Jack cheese
6 (no-boil) lasagna noodles

In a large bowl, mix the first 6 ingredients (remember to reserve 2 cups of cheese for layering). In a 9"x13" pan, spread 2 cups of chicken mixture. Place 3 of the uncooked noodles (2 horizontally and 1 vertically) on top of mixture; add 2 more cups of chicken mixture and 1 cup cheese sprinkle on top. Continue with 3 more noodles, 2 cups chicken mixture, and 1 cup cheese for the top. Bake at 350° for 45 minutes. Serves 8.

Joan Murray

Desserts

Ann's Coconut Cream Cake
Apple Pie
Apricot Bars
Autumn Torte
Bananas Foster
Bittersweet Chocolate Torte
Blueberry Cake
Blueberry Sour Cream Pie
Brandy-topped Peach Pie
Brownies with Nuts
Buster Bar Dessert
Butterscotch Apple Crumb Pie
Cheese Shortbreads
Cherry Pudding
Chocolate Angel Layers
Chocolate Bread Pudding with Cointreau Sauce
Chocolate Chip Bars
Chocolate Cranberry Cake
Chocolate Frango
Chocolate Mousse
Chocolate Mousse Pie
Chocolate Silk Pie
Chocolate Sour Cream Cake
Chocolate Zucchini Cake
Coffee Soufflé
Cranberry Bread Pudding
Date Nut Macaroon Pie
Easy Sticky Cinnamon Buns
"Encore" Crème Brûlée
Fabulous Pound Cake
French Apple Cake
Fresh Apple Cake
German Sweet Chocolate Pie
Harvey Wallbanger Cake
Hot Fudge Sauce
Indestructible Grand Marnier Soufflé
Indiana Hay Stacks
Irish Coffee Pie
Lady Finger Torte
Lemon Pie
Lime Meringue Pie
Luscious Cherry Crisp
Mamo's Blueberry Buckle

Maple Sauce
The Maramor Chocolate Sauce
Meringue Cookies
Mocha Pot de Crème
Mom's Strawberry Pie
Mother Joe's Pound Cake
Mother's Cheesecake
Mother's Lemon Cake
Neapolitan Refrigerator Dessert
Oatmeal Chocolate Raisin Cookies
Oatmeal Lace Cookies
Peach & Blueberry Crisp
Pears in Red Wine
Pecan Pie
Perfect Apple Pie
Pound Cake
Pumpkin Chiffon
Raspberry Chocolate Cake
Rugelach
Rum Cake
Sand Tarts
Seven Layer Cake
Strawberries with Mascarpone Cheese
Swedish Nuts
Tiramisu Lite
Toni's Walnut Cake
Venetian Biscotti
Viennese Brownies
Vinegar Pie

Ann's Coconut Cream Cake

2 eggs
1/2 cup heavy cream
1 cup cake flour
1 cup sugar
1 teaspoon baking powder

Topping:
3 tablespoons butter
5 tablespoons brown sugar
1 cup angel flake shredded
coconut
2 tablespoons heavy cream

Preheat oven to 350°. Break 2 eggs into a 1-cup measuring cup. Fill the rest with heavy cream. Pour into a mixing bowl and stir until blended. In another bowl, sift together cake flour, sugar and baking powder. Then add to egg and cream mixture. Beat well with an electric mixer until batter is very smooth. Pour batter into a well-greased 8"x8" baking pan and bake for 25-30 minutes or until done. While cake is baking, prepare the topping. Melt butter in saucepan, then add brown sugar and stir until sugar is dissolved, but do not allow to boil. Add shredded coconut to the butter and sugar mixture and stir until all the coconut is coated. Then add 2 tablespoons of heavy cream and mix well. Set aside. Allow the cake to cool for 5 minutes. Then spread the topping evenly over the surface of the cake with a knife or the back of a large spoon. Set your oven to broil and place the cake on a rack about 5-6 inches away from the heat source and broil the topping for about 3-4 minutes, or until topping gets bubbly and golden brown. Be sure to watch the topping very carefully, as it could burn very quickly under the broiler. Remove the cake from the broiler and allow to cool completely. Cut into squares with a sharp serrated knife. Serves 9-12.

Double the ingredients for a 13"x9" cake.

Ann Cardamone

Apple Pie

Pastry for 2 crusts
(9-inch pies)
6-8 MacIntosh apples
1 cup sugar
2 teaspoons cinnamon
1 tablespoon flour

21/2 tablespoons lemon juice
1 teaspoon finely chopped
lemon peel
1 tablespoon butter
1/2 cup confectioner's sugar

Peel and slice apples and put into crust. Pour over the apples, sugar, cinnamon, flour, 1 tablespoon lemon juice and lemon peel. Dot with butter. Place crust over pie. Bake in 425° oven for 15 minutes and 325° for 45 minutes. While still hot, pour or brush glaze of 11/2 tablespoon lemon juice mixed with confectioner's sugar over top of pie. Serves 8.

Dolores Lyon

Apricot Bars

Crust:
1/2 cup butter
1/4 cup sugar
1 cup flour

Filling:
1/3 cup flour

1/2 teaspoon baking powder
1/4 teaspoon salt
1 cup light brown sugar
2 eggs, beaten
1/2 teaspoon vanilla
1/2 cup dried apricots, chopped
1/2 cup chopped walnuts

Preheat oven to 350°. Using a pastry blender, cut butter into dry ingredients until crumbly. Press dough into an 8-inch square pan. Bake for 20 minutes. Remove from oven. Filling: Beat together first 6 ingredients. Chop apricots and steam them in a small amount of water (just enough water to cover the bottom of the pan). Apricots should be soft. Blend nuts and apricots into filling mixture. Pour into baked crust. Bake for 30 minutes. Cool and cut into small bars. Roll in confectioner's sugar. Yields 36 bars.

Jennifer Buschi

Autumn Torte

1/2 cup butter or margarine

2 cups granulated sugar

2 beaten eggs

7 medium apples, finely chopped

1 cup walnuts, chopped

2 cups flour

2 teaspoons baking soda

1 teaspoon nutmeg

1 teaspoon cinnamon

3/4 teaspoon salt

1 teaspoon vanilla (optional)

Sauce:

1/2 cup butter

1/2 cup Half and Half

1/2 cup granulated sugar

1/2 cup brown sugar

Cream together first 3 ingredients. Mix in apples and walnuts. Sift and add next 5 ingredients (flour through salt). Place in greased and floured 9"x13" cake pan. Bake 30-45 minutes in preheated 350° oven. Cut in squares and top with the hot sauce. To make sauce: Cook together butter, Half and Half, granulated and brown sugars in saucepan until smooth and well blended. Add vanilla just before serving, if desired. Serves 15.

Kristen Sonneborn

Bananas Foster

6 tablespoons butter

1/2 cup firmly packed brown sugar

1/2 teaspoon cinnamon

4 bananas, halved lengthwise

1/2 cup banana-flavored liqueur

3/4 cup rum

1 pint vanilla ice cream

Melt butter in a chafing dish. Add sugar and cinnamon. Cook syrup over medium heat until bubbly. Add bananas and heat 3-4 minutes, basting constantly with syrup. Combine liqueur and rum in a small long-handled pan. Heat just until warm. Ignite with a long match and pour over bananas. Baste bananas with sauce until flames die down. Serve immediately over ice cream. Serves 4.

Judie Grossman

Bittersweet Chocolate Torte

A potato peeler works well for shaving hard chocolate.

2 sticks unsalted butter

3 ounces unsweetened chocolate

6 ounces semi-sweet chocolate

4 extra large eggs

1 1/4 cups sugar

1 tablespoon flour

Topping (optional):

Heavy whipping cream, whipped, flavored with a little sugar and vanilla

Raspberries for garnish

Preheat oven to 325°. Melt butter and chocolate together, allowing to cool. Combine eggs and sugar. Beat until light. Add flour. Add melted chocolate mixture, stirring well. Pour into 8-inch springform pan that has been lightly greased and sprinkled with a little sugar to lightly coat the sides. Wrap the pan with aluminum foil, leaving top exposed. Place pan in larger Pyrex baking dish. Pour boiling water into the larger pan to a depth of about 1 inch. Do not let the edge of the springform touch the rim of the outer pan. Bake at 325° for 1 hour. Remove springform pan from water bath and place on wire rack. Allow to cool before removing chocolate torte. Slice pieces and serve on individual plates. Serves 8-10.

Phyllis Liebman

Blueberry Cake

2 eggs, separated
1 cup sugar
1/2 cup shortening
1/4 teaspoon salt
1 teaspoon vanilla

1 1/2 cups sifted flour
1 teaspoon baking powder
1/3 cup milk
1 1/2 cups fresh blueberries

Beat egg whites until stiff; add about 1/4 cup sugar to keep them stiff. Cream shortening, add salt and vanilla to this. Add remaining sugar gradually. Add unbeaten egg yolks and beat until light and creamy. Add sifted dry ingredients alternately with the milk. Fold in beaten whites. Fold in the fresh blueberries. (First take a bit of the flour called for in the recipe and gently shake berries in it so they won't settle.) Turn into a greased 8"x8" pan. Sprinkle top of batter lightly with granulated sugar. Bake at 350° for 50-60 minutes. Serves 8.

Marcia Kelley

When a cake recipe calls for flouring the baking pan, use a bit of the dry cake mix instead and there won't be any white mess on the outside of the cake.

Blueberry Sour Cream Pie

2 1/2 cups blueberries
3 tablespoons sugar
1/4 teaspoon cinnamon
1/8 teaspoon salt
Pinch of nutmeg

3 eggs
1 cup sour cream
1/4 cup honey
1/4 cup sugar
1 pre-made pie crust

In a large bowl, toss blueberries with the sugar mixture (sugar, cinnamon, salt and nutmeg). In a small bowl, beat 3 eggs with sour cream, honey and sugar. Add the custard mixture to berries and mix them gently together. Pour filling into the pre-made pie shell and bake at 325° for 1 hour. Serve warm. Serves 8.

Susan Stevens

Brandy-topped Peach Pie

6-8 peaches, peeled and halved
1 (9 inch) pie shell, partially
   baked
1 cup sugar
1/3 cup butter
1/3 cup flour
1 egg, beaten

1/4 teaspoon vanilla

Topping:
2 ounces peach brandy
1 ounce triple sec
1/2 cup cream cheese, softened
   at room temperature

Preheat oven to 425°. Place peach halves in pie shell, cavity down. Cream sugar and butter. Add flour, egg and vanilla, mixing well. Spread mixture over peaches. Bake for 15 minutes. Reduce heat to 325° and bake for 60 minutes or until peaches are done. Put topping ingredients in blender. Blend until smooth. Pour 2 tablespoons over each slice of pie when served. Serves 8-10.

Jean Beaver

Brownies with Nuts

2 squares Baker's unsweetened chocolate

1 stick butter

2 whole eggs

1 cup sugar

3/4 cup flour

1/2 teaspoon salt

1/2 teaspoon baking powder

1 teaspoon vanilla

1 cup chopped walnuts

Preheat oven to 350°. Put 2 squares of chocolate on top of 1 stick of butter in medium-sized saucepan over very low heat, watching closely. Melt the butter and chocolate. Do not let it burn. While that is cooling, beat 2 eggs, add 1 cup sugar and beat well. Add salt, baking powder and vanilla. Add this mixture to the pan with melted butter and chocolate. Add flour and nuts. Bake at 350° in a 8"x8"x2" pan for 30 minutes. Serves 8-10.

Sally Frazier

Buster Bar Dessert

24 Oreo cookies, crushed

1/3 cup butter

1/2 gallon peppermint bon-bon ice cream, softened

11/2 cups roasted Spanish peanuts

1 can Hershey fudge topping, heated

1 (8 ounce) container Cool Whip

Mix crushed cookies and butter. Place in a 9"x13" pan and freeze for 1/2 hour. Spread ice cream on top. Place peanuts on top of ice cream and freeze for 1/2 hour. Pour the fudge topping over the ice cream and peanuts. Freeze for 1/2 hour. Add the Cool Whip as the final layer. Freeze. Take out 15 minutes before serving to aid in cutting. Serves 10-12.

Sharon Wilson

A sheet of baker's parchment on a cookie sheet yields evenly baked cookies. It is better than greasing with vegetable shortening. Butter and oil will cause cookies to burn.

Butterscotch Apple Crumb Pie

1 1/2 teaspoons lemon juice

4 cups pared, cubed and
sliced tart cooking apples

1/2 cup sugar

1/4 cup all-purpose flour

1 teaspoon cinnamon

1/8 teaspoon salt

1 (9 inch) unbaked pie shell

Topping:

1 cup butterscotch morsels

1/4 cup butter

3/4 cup all-purpose flour

1/8 teaspoon salt

Preheat oven to 375°. In a large bowl, combine lemon juice and apples. Toss until well coated. Stir in sugar, flour, cinnamon and salt. Mix well. Turn into unbaked pie shell. Cover edges with aluminum foil. Bake for 20 minutes. To make the topping, melt the butterscotch morsels and butter over hot (not boiling) water. Stir until smooth. Remove foil from pie. Pour mixture over top of hot apples. Bake for an additional 20-25 minutes. Makes one 9-inch pie. Serves 8.

Dianne Sponseller

Cheese Shortbreads

1/2 pound well-aged, grated
   cheddar cheese
1/4 pound softened butter
1/2 teaspoon salt

11/4 cups flour
Dash of dry mustard
Dash of cayenne

Combine all the ingredients above. Work until smooth and form into a cylinder, 1" in diameter. Wrap in foil and chill. Slice like refrigerator cookies 1/4" thick, then bake at 350° for 10 minutes, or until lightly colored.

Pat Hartmann

These little cheese pastries are good nibbling with a preprandial glass of Champagne or dry Sherry, or with a mellow Sherry at teatime.

Cherry Pudding

1 cup canned sour pitted or
   canned bing cherries, drained
1/2 cup shortening
1 teaspoon vanilla
1 cup dry bread crumbs
1/2 cup sugar

Pinch of salt (optional)
3 eggs, separated
1/2 cup juice from cherries
1/4 cup sugar
1/2 cup red sweet wine

Squeeze juice from cherries and set both aside. Cream together shortening, sugar, salt and vanilla. Add egg yolks one at a time. Fold in bread crumbs, cherries and egg whites that have been stiffly beaten. Place mixture in a well greased deep casserole or bundt pan. Place in a pan of water and bake at 350° for 1 hour. Let rest for 15-20 minutes. Turn onto platter and serve with sauce. To make the sauce, mix last 3 ingredients together and bring to a boil to thicken. Serves 8-10.

Suzanne Parelman

Chocolate Angel Layers

If chocolate angel food cake mix is not available, use regular angel food cake mix. Slowly and carefully fold in 3 rounded tablespoons cocoa into batter by hand. Bake as directed.

1 chocolate angel food cake mix

1 (6 ounce) package semi-sweet chocolate chips

1/4 pound large marshmallows, about 16

1/2 cup milk

1 cup heavy cream, whipped

Prepare angel food cake mix according to package directions in an ungreased tube pan. Cool. Cut cake cross-wise in 2 equal layers. Prepare frosting in double boiler by combining chocolate chips, marshmallows and milk. Cover and heat over simmering water until blended. Stirring occasionally. Cool. Stir until smooth. Whip 1 cup cream and fold in. Place small layer of frosting between cake halves. Frost cake with remaining mixture. Chill for 45 minutes or until frosting sets. Serves 8-12.

Kristen Sonneborn

Chocolate Bread Pudding with Cointreau Sauce

1 loaf French bread

3 eggs beaten

1 quart milk

2 cups sugar

2 tablespoons vanilla

1/2 cup raisins (optional)

3 squares unsweetened chocolate, melted

1/2 cup roasted chopped hazelnuts

Tear the French bread into 1-inch pieces and place in a large bowl. Combine eggs, milk, sugar and vanilla. Pour the mixture over the bread, stir in the raisins, chocolate and hazelnuts. Let soak for 30 minutes. Bake in a buttered 8"x8" pan, placed in 2" of water, at 350° for 1 hour. Serves 8.

Cointreau Sauce:

8 tablespoons butter

1 egg, beaten

1 cup sugar

1/2 cup Cointreau (or orange liqueur)

Dissolve sugar in the butter in a saucepan over low heat (mixture will be bubbly). Remove pan from stove and when the bubbling has stopped, stir in beaten egg and Cointreau. Pour over individual servings of pudding.

Patricia Dirks

Chocolate Chip Bars

Pecans are usually my favorite nuts in cookies; however, English walnuts taste great in this recipe. This is a real favorite.

3 sticks butter, softened
21/4 cups light brown sugar
1 teaspoon vanilla
3 large eggs
1 cup flour
11/2 teaspoons baking powder
1 teaspoon salt
1 teaspoon cinnamon
11/4 cups oatmeal, quick cooking
12 ounces chocolate chips, semi-sweet
11/2 cups nuts, chopped (pecans or English walnuts)

Cream butter with brown sugar until light and fluffy. Then add vanilla and eggs. Continue to beat with mixer until light. Add dry ingredients. Stir in chocolate chips and nuts. Bake in greased 9"x13" pan at 350° for approximately 25 minutes. Cut into squares. Freezes well. Serves 10-12.

Frances Luessenhop

Chocolate Cranberry Cake

2 cups all-purpose flour

3/4 cup sugar

3/4 cup oil

3 eggs

2 teaspoons vanilla extract

1 teaspoon baking soda

1/2 teaspoon cinnamon

1/8 teaspoon salt

1 (16 ounce) can whole cranberry sauce

1 (6 ounce) package semi-sweet chocolate morsels

1 cup chopped walnuts

Preheat oven to 350°. Combine flour, sugar, oil, eggs, vanilla, baking soda, cinnamon and salt. Mix well. Stir in cranberry sauce, chocolate morsels and nuts. Pour into greased and floured 9-cup bundt pan or a 10-inch tube pan. Remove and cool completely. Sprinkle top with powdered sugar, if desired. Serves 8-10.

Flo Chelm

Chocolate Frango

1 cup unsalted butter

2 cups powdered sugar

Pinch of salt

4 squares unsweetened
chocolate, melted

4 whole eggs

3/4 teaspoon peppermint
extract

2 teaspoons pure vanilla extract

1/2 cup finely chopped pecans

1 cup graham cracker crumbs

Whipped cream

Mix butter, sugar and salt. Add remaining ingredients, adding eggs 1 at a time. Put 1 teaspoon of graham cracker crumbs in a 21/2-inch in diameter double baking cups. Use a muffin tin to keep paper cup in shape. Fill with mixture. Top with more crumbs if desired. Freeze. Makes 13 cups. Serve frozen. Top with dollop of whipped cream.

Virginia Andrews-Dibeler

Chocolate Mousse

8 ounces sweet chocolate

8 ounces unsweetened
chocolate

5 egg whites

1 cup sugar

1 teaspoon vanilla

2 cups whipping cream,
whipped

Coffee liqueur (optional)

Melt both chocolates in top double boiler over hot—not boiling water. Beat egg whites until soft white peaks form and then gradually beat in sugar and then vanilla. Beat until smooth and peaks stand almost straight. Mix melted chocolate carefully into egg whites along with whipped cream. Fold together until blended. Turn into a very lightly oiled 5 or 6 cup mold of a simple shape or mold in a serving dish. Chill at least 2 hours or until firm. Unmold, if necessary, using warm water to loosen. Serve with coffee liqueur in separate pitcher for people to pour over as desired. Serves 12-16.

Mickey Baumgartner

Chocolate Mousse Pie

1 (6 ounce) package semi-sweet chocolate pieces

2 egg whites

1 cup heavy cream

1 egg

2 egg yolks

1 teaspoon rum or sherry

1 square unsweetened chocolate, shaved

Crust:

11/3 graham cracker crumbs

1/3 cup brown sugar

1/2 teaspoon cinnamon

1/3 cup melted butter

Melt chocolate pieces over hot, not boiling water. (Be careful not to get water in chocolate.) Beat egg whites until they peak when beater is raised. Whip cream. Beat whole egg and egg yolks together until thick and lemon colored. Mix rum into eggs. Remove chocolate pieces from heat. Beat a little warm chocolate into eggs, so they won't cook. Add remaining chocolate to eggs and mix well. Fold beaten whites and cream into chocolate mixture. Refrigerate until chilled. Crust: Mix all ingredients. Press to bottom and sides of well-greased 9-inch pie pan. Spoon mixture into shell. Shave unsweetened chocolate on top. Serves 6-8.

Carrie Petty

Chocolate Silk Pie

1/2 cup butter, softened

3/4 cup granulated sugar

1 (1 ounce) square unsweetened chocolate, melted and cooled

1 teaspoon vanilla

2 eggs, divided

Prepared graham cracker crust

Sweetened whipped cream

Cream butter and gradually add sugar, beating at medium speed with an electric mixer until the butter and sugar are well blended. Stir in chocolate and vanilla. Add 1 of the eggs and beat with the mixer for 4 minutes. Add the other egg and beat for 5 more minutes. Spoon this mixture into a graham cracker crust and chill for at least 8 hours. Serve with sweetened whipped cream. Serves 8.

Marcia Kelley

Chocolate Sour Cream Cake

A county fair blue ribbon winner!

1/2 pound unsalted butter

11/2 cups sugar

5 extra large eggs

1 cup sour cream

2 teaspoons baking powder

1 teaspoon baking soda

1 teaspoon vanilla

3 cups flour

Dash of salt

1 cup chocolate chips

Topping:

2 squares unsweetened chocolate

1 cup sugar

2 tablespoons cinnamon

Preheat oven to 350°. Grease and flour tube pan. Cream butter and sugar. Add eggs, sour cream, baking powder, baking soda, vanilla and salt. Blend in flour. Fold in chocolate chips. In tube pan layer 1/2 batter and 1/2 topping: repeat. Topping: Melt unsweetend chocolate. Stir in sugar and cinnamon. Serves 10-12.

Sandra Stone

Chocolate Zucchini Cake

Butter for greasing pan
3 squares baking chocolate
3 cups unsifted flour
1 teaspoon baking soda
11/2 teaspoons baking powder
1 teaspoon salt

4 eggs
3 cups sugar
11/2 cups canola oil
3 cups grated zucchini
1 cup chopped walnuts

Preheat oven to 350°. Melt chocolate and let cool slightly. Grease 10-inch bundt pan. Mix together flour, baking soda, baking powder and salt. Mix eggs at a high speed until thick and light. Gradually add sugar and oil to eggs. Beat well. Mix zucchini, nuts and chocolate and stir. Add dry ingredients and stir well, but don't beat. Bake at 350° for 1 hour to 1 hour and 15 minutes. Check for doneness. Let cool for 20 minutes, then turn out onto a cake rack to cool completely. Dust with confectioner's sugar. Makes 1-2 loaves.

Alice Blum

Can be made in 2 large loaf pans and the baking time will be slightly less. Delicious, easy cake— very moist and chocolaty.

Coffee Soufflé

Enjoy dessert after a heavy dinner: fresh berries covered with French vanilla cream or Irish Crème.

11/2 cups coffee
1 tablespoon unflavored gelatin
2/3 cup sugar, divided
1/2 cup milk

3 eggs, separated
1/4 teaspoon salt
1/2 teaspoon vanilla
Whipped cream

Combine coffee, gelatin, 1/3 cup sugar and milk in top of boiler. Lightly beat egg yolks. Mix with remaining 1/3 cup sugar and salt. Add to liquid in double boiler, mixing well. Cook over simmering water until thickened and smooth. Beat egg whites with vanilla. Fold into cooked sauce. Pour mixture into mold. Chill until firm. Serve with dollops of whipped cream. Serves 6.

Ann Helmsderfer

Cranberry Bread Pudding

1 loaf raisin bread, broken into 1-inch pieces
3 cups light cream
1 cup cranberry sauce

1 orange rind, finely grated
3 eggs, beaten
1/2 cup sugar
2 teaspoons pure vanilla extract

Soak bread in cream for 1 hour. Mix in the remaining ingredients and pour into a buttered 2-quart baking dish. Bake in a preheated 350° oven for 1 hour, or until knife inserted into the center comes out clean. Serve warm or cold with heavy cream, whipped cream, or vanilla ice cream, if desired. Serves 8-10.

Dianne Sponseller

Date Nut Macaroon Pie

12 saltine crackers, crushed
12 dates, chopped fine
1/2 cup chopped nuts
1/2 teaspoon baking powder
3 egg whites, beaten stiff

1 teaspoon water
1/2 teaspoon almond extract
1 cup sugar
Whipped cream for garnish

Crush saltines. Add chopped dates, chopped nuts and baking powder. Set aside. Beat egg whites, water and almond extract until soft peaks form. Gradually add sugar and beat until stiff. Fold date and nut mixture into egg white mixture. Spread into buttered pie plate and bake for 35 minutes at 325°. Chill and garnish with whipped cream. Serves 8.

Maria Waine

Easy Sticky Cinnamon Buns

2 loaves frozen bread dough, thawed
1 cup raisins
1 cup chopped nuts
11/2 cups brown sugar
3/4 cup butter or margarine
2 small packages vanilla pudding (not instant)
3 tablespoons milk
1 tablespoon cinnamon

Cut thawed dough into 15 slices for each loaf. Cover bottom of two 9"x13" pans with raisins and nuts. Lay 5 slices of dough in each pan. Melt brown sugar, butter, pudding and milk. Stir until mixed well. Pour over slices and sprinkle with cinnamon. Cover and let rise in warm place for 3 hours. Bake in preheated oven at 350° for 30 minutes. Turn out on tray immediately. Serves 12-15.

Colleen Brennan

"Encore" Crème Brûlée

1 pint whipping cream
1 pint Half and Half
8 egg yolks
3 tablespoons sugar
2 teaspoons vanilla
1/2 teaspoon salt
3/4 cup brown sugar

Scald whipping cream and Half and Half. Beat egg yolks and add sugar, vanilla and salt. Slowly pour hot creams into egg mixture. Pour into 14"x9" pan. Bake in hot water for 1 hour. Cool. Chill in refrigerator. Put brown sugar on top and broil 6-8 minutes. Serves 8.

Mrs. Nelson Hagan

Fabulous Pound Cake

1 1/2 cups (3 sticks) unsalted butter

3 cups granulated sugar

6 large brown eggs

1 cup sour cream

3 cups all-purpose flour

1/2 teaspoon baking soda

1/4 teaspoon salt

1 teaspoon vanilla extract

Cakes freeze very well. If carefully wrapped, will keep fresh for many weeks.

Cream butter in electric mixer until it reaches the consistency of heavy cream. Add eggs. Slowly add sugar, 1 tablespoon at a time, beating well. Stir in sour cream. Put measured flour in a sifter with baking soda and salt. Sift 3 times. Add sifted flour to the creamed mixture, 1/2 cup at a time; beat to combine thoroughly. Add vanilla and mix well. Pour batter into 3 carefully buttered 8"x3 3/4"x2 1/2" disposable aluminum loaf pans, distributing batter evenly. Arrange pans on an aluminum cookie sheet and bake in a preheated oven at 325° for 1 hour or until cakes test done. Cool 15 minutes on rack before turning cakes out to cool completely. Makes 2 loaves.

Vernon Dibeler

French Apple Cake

3/4 cup vegetable oil

1/2 cup softened butter

2 cups sugar

2 eggs

3 cups apples, chopped and peeled

1 cup walnuts, chopped

3 cups flour

1 teaspoon salt

1 teaspoon cinnamon

1 teaspoon baking soda

2 teaspoons vanilla

Combine oil, butter, sugar, eggs, apples and nuts. Blend well. Sift flour, salt, cinnamon and soda. Blend well and add to the above. Add vanilla and stir. Place in 9"x13" baking pan. Bake for 50-60 minutes at 350°. Cover with confectioner's sugar, whipped cream, or ice cream. Serves 10.

Lisa Crowder

Fresh Apple Cake

4 cups Granny Smith apples

2 cups granulated sugar

1/2 cup canola oil

1 cup raisins

1 cup chopped walnuts

2 eggs, well beaten

1 teaspoon vanilla

2 cups all purpose flour

2 teaspoons baking soda

1 teaspoon cinnamon

1 teaspoon salt

Glaze:

1 cup confectioners sugar

1 teaspoon vanilla

2 tablespoons water

Peel, core and chop apples. Add sugar, oil, raisins, nuts, eggs and vanilla. Sift dry ingredients and mix in with moist mixture. Place in 13"x9"x2" pan. Bake at 350° for 1 hour or until toothpick comes out clean. Mix confectioners sugar, vanilla and water to make the glaze. Drizzle cake with glaze. Cut into squares. Serves 16.

Sally Lopez

German Sweet Chocolate Pie

1 (4 ounce) package German sweet chocolate

1/2 cup milk

2 tablespoons sugar

1 (3 ounce) package cream cheese, softened

3 1/2 cups Cool Whip, thawed

1 graham cracker crust

Heat chocolate and 2 tablespoons of milk in a saucepan over low heat, stirring until chocolate is melted. Beat sugar into cream cheese. Add remaining milk and chocolate mixture. Beat until smooth. Fold in whipped topping, blending until smooth. Spoon into crust. Freeze until firm. Garnish. Let stand at room temperature to soften before serving. Serves 8.

Roberta Camarota

Harvey Wallbanger Cake

1 box yellow cake mix	Topping:
1 box vanilla pudding	1 stick butter
3/4 cup vegetable oil	1 cup sugar
4 eggs	1/4 cup orange juice
1/4 cup vodka	1/4 cup Galliano
1/4 cup Galliano	
2/3 cup orange juice	

Keeps well refrigerated. Can add a dollop of whipped cream and sliced strawberries.

Mix cake and pudding mix. Add next 5 ingredients. Beat well for about 2 minutes. Pour into buttered bundt pan. Bake at 350° for 45 minutes or until cake tested comes out clean or top springs back when lightly pressed. To make the topping, mix butter, sugar and orange juice in a small saucepan and boil 3 minutes, then add Galliano at last 1/2 minute to retain flavor. Cool 30 minutes in pan and pour 1/3 the topping on the cake. Let cool another 1/2 hour and remove from pan. Pour rest of topping on cake. Serves 8-10.

Vilma Novak

Hot Fudge Sauce

You'll never use store-bought again!

1 cup sugar

1 cup Karo syrup

1/2 cup cocoa

1/2 cup Half and Half or

evaporated milk

3 tablespoons butter

1 pinch salt

1 teaspoon vanilla extract

Combine all but vanilla in saucepan. Cook over medium heat, stirring constantly, until mixture comes to a full rolling boil. Boil briskly for another 3 minutes stirring occasionally. Remove from heat and add vanilla. Serve warm. Keep in refrigerator and warm in microwave. Serves 8-10.

Jeanne Drackett

Indestructible Grand Marnier Soufflé

3 tablespoons butter

3 tablespoons flour

1/4 teaspoon salt

1/4 cup whole milk

4 eggs, separated

1/2 teaspoon cream of tartar

1/2 cup Grand Marnier

Grated orange peel

1/2 cup sugar

Butter 4 individual serving ramekins and dust with sugar and set aside. In medium saucepan, over medium heat, melt butter and blend in flour and salt. Cook, stirring constantly, until mixture is smooth and bubbly. Should have a thick, creamy consistency. Stir in all of the milk at once. Cook, stirring constantly, until mixture boils and is smooth and thickened. Set aside. In a large mixing bowl, beat egg whites with cream of tartar at high speed until foamy. Add sugar slowly until dissolved and whites are glossy and stand in soft peaks. Set aside. Blend egg yolks, Grand Marnier and orange peel into the butter/flour roux made earlier. When mixed thoroughly, fold this mixture into the egg whites. Pour into individual ramekins filling about 3/4 to the top. Bake in a water bath at 350° for 45-55 minutes until puffy and delicately browned on top. May be dusted with confectioners sugar. Serves 4.

Lois & Alan Lang

Indiana Hay Stacks

1 (11 ounce) Nestle
Butterscotch Morsels
1 (5 ounce) can La Chow
Mein Noodles

1 (9.25 ounce) can Planter's
cashews, halves and pieces

Melt butterscotch bits in double boiler at medium-low heat. Stir in at medium-high until melted. Add noodles and nuts. Spread on cookie sheet. Mix well and refrigerate. Break into pieces. Serves 6-8.

Phyllis Harris

Irish Coffee Pie

Crust:
1 cup sifted all-purpose flour
1/2 cup margarine
2 tablespoons sugar
1/4 teaspoons salt

3/4 cup coffee
3 tablespoons Irish whiskey
1 carton whipping cream
Cool Whip
Shaved chocolate

Filling:
1 (31/2 ounce) vanilla instant
pudding

To make the crust: mix flour, margarine, sugar and salt until crumbly. Press into a greased 9-inch pie plate, and bake at 375° for 12-15 minutes. Make pudding per package directions and add coffee in mixer bowl and beat at high speed for 1 minute. Beat the whipped cream and add small amount of sugar and fold into pudding mix. Pile it into baked pastry shell and chill for several hours. Before serving, spread Cool Whip over entire pie, garnished with shaved chocolate. Serves 8.

Janice Brinkman

The Art of Cooking • Desserts

Ladyfinger Torte

3 packages ladyfingers
(use 1/2 sections at a time)
1 (8 ounce) and 1 (3 ounce)
cream cheese
1 cup sugar

1 teaspoon vanilla
1 pint all-purpose cream
1 can pie filling, i.e.
strawberry, cherry, pineapple
(your choice)

Butter springform pan. Layer sides and bottom with ladyfingers. Whip cream cheese, sugar and vanilla. Whip cream to fold into cream cheese mixture. Pour 1/2 filling into pan. Add another layer of ladyfingers, then rest of filling. Top with pie filling. Chill overnight and serve. Serves 8-10.

Lynn Cole

Lemon Pie

1-2 slices white bread
1 (8 inch) pie shell, baked
3/4 cup butter
1 cup sugar
1-2 tablespoons grated lemon peel

Juice of 2 lemons and the rind, grated
3 eggs, separated
1 whole egg
6 tablespoons sugar

Cut crusts from bread. Tear or cut bread into large cubes. Arrange evenly in baked pie shell. Melt butter over low heat; stir in 1 cup sugar, lemon rind and juice. Heat until sugar dissolves. Beat egg yolks and whole egg together. Stir into lemon mixture. Cook and stir until mixture thickens. Do not boil. Heat oven to 350°. Beat egg whites until frothy; gradually add 6 tablespoons sugar. Beat until stiff and glossy. Spoon hot mixture over bread in crust. Cover with meringue. Bake until light brown. Cool and serve at room temperature. Serves 8.

Marian Lacy

Lime Meringue Pie

1 1/2 cups sugar

7 tablespoons cornstarch

2 cups boiling water

5 egg yolks, beaten

2 lemon rinds, grated

1/4 teaspoon salt

1/2 cup unstrained lime or
   key lime juice

5 egg whites

1/4 teaspoon salt

8-10 tablespoons sugar

1 prepared pie crust

Sift sugar with cornstarch into the top of a double boiler. Pour in 2 cups boiling water. Stir mixture to smooth consistency for 5 minutes. Stir in beaten egg yolks, rind of 2 lemons, salt and unstrained lime juice. Cool the filling and pour into the pie crust. For meringue, beat egg whites with salt until stiff. Add sugar until well blended. Spread evenly on top of filling. Bake at 300° until browned. Serves 8.

Maggie Lauer

When slicing meringue pie, run the knife through butter before slicing and it will prevent the meringue from sticking to the knife. It will make a nice clean cut.

Luscious Cherry Crisp

3 cups canned dark pitted
  bing cherries, drained

2/3 cup packed brown sugar

1/2 cup all-purpose flour

1/2 cup all-purpose oats

1/3 cup butter (or margarine),
  softened

3/4 teaspoon ground cinnamon

3/4 teaspoon ground nutmeg

Preheat oven to 375° and grease 8"x8"x2" pan.
Spread cherries in pan. Combine sugar, flour, oats,
butter, cinnamon and nutmeg. Sprinkle over cherries.
Bake about 30 minutes or until top is golden. Serve
with vanilla ice cream, if desired. Serves 6.

Leslie Branda

Mamo's Blueberry Buckle

1/4 cup butter, softened
1/4 cup sugar
1 teaspoon vanilla flavoring
1 teaspoon almond flavoring
1 egg
1 teaspoon baking powder
11/3 cups flour
1/2 teaspoon salt

1/3 cup whole milk
2 cups blueberries

Streusel mixture:
1/2 cup sugar
1/3 cup flour
1/4 cup soft butter

Cream butter and sugar. Add vanilla and almond flavorings and egg. Mix together. Combine salt, baking powder, and 1 cup flour. Add to creamed mixture alternating with milk. Pour into 8"x8" greased pan and top with blueberries. Scatter streusel mixture (last 3 ingredients) over the top and bake at 375° for 45 minutes. Serves 8.

Anne Steffen

Maple Sauce

11/2 cups packed light brown sugar

2/3 cup maple syrup

1/4 cup unsalted butter

1 small can evaporated milk

Bring brown sugar, maple syrup and butter to a boil in a medium saucepan over medium-high heat. Simmer for 5 minutes. Remove, cool slightly, then stir in evaporated milk, blending well. Store in the refrigerator. Just before serving, warm slightly and ladle over ice cream or choice of dessert. If desired, sprinkle toasted, chopped pecans on top. Makes 21/2 cups.

Marcia Kelley

The Maramor Chocolate Sauce

Fun dessert: Fill small flower pots with ice-cream, placing a straw down the middle, then top with chocolate sauce and put a flower in the straw.

1/2 cup melted butter (no margarine)

8 squares Baker's unsweetened chocolate

3 cups sugar

2 heaping tablespoons cornstarch

Pinch of salt

1/2 cup light Karo syrup

1 large can Carnation milk

1 teaspoon vanilla

Melt butter and chocolate in top of double boiler. Add other ingredients except vanilla and cook until smooth. Remove from heat and add 1 teaspoon vanilla. Can be stored in refrigerator in a tightly closed jar for several weeks. Warm before serving over ice cream or gingerbread. Makes 1 cup.

Shirle Krueger

Meringue Cookies

2 egg whites
2/3 cup sugar
1 teaspoon vanilla

1 cup chopped walnuts
1 small bag chocolate chips

Preheat oven to 350°. Beat egg whites until soft; gradually add sugar until stiff. Stir in vanilla. Add walnuts and chocolate chips. Line 2 cookie sheets with foil. Drop teaspoons of egg whites on cookie sheets. Put in oven. Turn off heat and leave overnight. Makes 2 dozen cookies.

Ethel Williams

Mocha Pot de Crème

6 ounces German sweet
chocolate
4 tablespoons sugar
Pinch of salt
1 egg
1 teaspoon vanilla extract

1 teaspoon instant coffee
1/4 cup Kahlua
11/2 cups medium cream,
heated to boiling
1 cup sweetened whipped
cream

Place all ingredients, except whipped cream, in blender. Pour hot cream over to cover. Blend for 1 minute. Pour immediately into pot de crème dishes and chill. After it begins to stiffen, then transfer to serving dishes. Serve either topped with whipped cream or fold whipped cream into mixture before pouring into dishes. Serves 4.

Claire DeSilver

Mom's Strawberry Pie

1 (9 inch) pie shell, baked
   and cooled
1 quart strawberries
3/4 to 1 cup sugar
2 tablespoons cornstarch

1/4 cup water
1 tablespoon butter
1 teaspoon lemon juice
Whipped cream or Cool Whip
   for garnish

Wash, hull and dry larger berries and line bottom of cooled pie shell. Place remaining berries in saucepan with sugar, cornstarch, water, butter and lemon juice. Simmer slowly, until mixture thickens about 8 to 10 minutes. Cool. Pour glaze over berries in pie shell. Chill until ready to serve. Garnish with whipped cream or cool whip. Blueberries or peaches may also be used. Serves 8.

Naomi Singer

Mother Joe's Pound Cake

1/2 pound butter
2 cups sugar
5 eggs, separated
2 cups flour

1 teaspoon baking powder
1/2 cup milk
1 teaspoon vanilla

Cream well together sugar and butter. Beat yolks of eggs well (adding 1 or 2 tablespoons water to yolks before you beat them) and add to the above mixture. Add flour and baking powder that have been sifted together, alternating with the milk. Add vanilla. Lastly, fold in well-beaten egg whites. Blend well. Bake for 45-50 minutes in a 350° oven using a buttered 9"x13"x2" pan. Serves 8.

Carole Nichols

Mother's Cheesecake

1 cooked graham cracker crust
12 ounces cream cheese
3/4 cup sugar
1 teaspoon vanilla

2 eggs, separated
1 pint sour cream
4 tablespoons sugar

Mix and cook your favorite graham cracker crust in a 10-inch pie plate. Heat cream cheese and sugar in a saucepan. Cool mixture and add vanilla and egg yolks. Fold in beaten egg whites. Bake at 325° for 25 minutes. Cool 10-15 minutes. Top cheesecake with a mixture of sour cream and sugar. Refrigerate. Serves 8.

Roxanne Powning

Mother's Lemon Cake

1 box yellow cake mix	Glaze:
1 box instant lemon pudding mix	2 cups powdered sugar
	1/2 cup lemon juice
4 eggs	4 teaspoons grated zest
3/4 cup vegetable oil	2 tablespoons oil
3/4 cup water	2 tablespoons water

Blend together first 5 ingredients. Grease lightly and flour 91/2"x13" baking dish or a bundt cake pan. Bake cake at 350° for 35 minutes or when top springs back. Mix glaze while cake is baking. While cake is still very warm, pour glaze slowly over the top. Serves 10-12.

Carolyn Davis

Neapolitan Refrigerator Dessert

1 frozen all-butter pound cake

2 cups whipping cream

2 tablespoons quick cocoa mix

3 tablespoons sugar (not all at once)

1 teaspoon vanilla

1/2 cup crushed frozen strawberries, thawed and drained

Fresh strawberries for garnish

Thaw cake and then cut into 4 lengthwise slices. Put bottom slice back into foil pan in which it came. Whip 1 cup of cream until stiff. Divide into 3 equal parts. To 1 part, add cocoa mix and 1 tablespoon sugar. Spread this over the bottom layer. Top with second layer. Mix 1 tablespoon sugar and vanilla with second portion of whipped cream. Spread over second layer of cake and top with third layer. Fold drained strawberries and third tablespoon of sugar into whipped cream. Spread over cake. Top with fourth layer and refrigerate several hours. When ready to serve, remove from foil, whip remaining cream and spread over entire cake. Garnish with pieces of fresh strawberries or something of your choice. Serves 6.

Dorothea Trump

Oatmeal Chocolate Raisin Cookies

Easy and fool-proof recipe — a hit with everyone!

3/4 cup butter
1 cup light brown sugar
2 eggs
1 tablespoon vanilla
1/2 teaspoon salt
11/2 cups flour

1 teaspoon soda
21/2 cups oatmeal
1/2 cup chopped pecans
1/2 package chocolate chips
1 cup raisins, soaked in
    boiling water and drained

Mix first 5 ingredients. Add next 5 ingredients. Mix well. Drain raisins and gently fold into mixture. Bake on ungreased cookie sheet at 350° for approximately 10 minutes. Makes approximately 20 cookies.

Sonja Laidig

Oatmeal Lace Cookies

This is an all-time family favorite, crisp, delicious and simple.

3/4 cup shortening or butter
1/2 cup brown sugar
1/2 cup white sugar, granulated
1 teaspoon vanilla
1/4 cup hot water

1 cup flour
3 cups oatmeal, plain
1/2 teaspoon salt
1/2 teaspoon baking soda

Cream shortening or butter, sugar and vanilla. Put soda in hot water to dissolve and add with the flour to the shortening. Mix 1 cup of oatmeal in mixer and the remainder by hand to incorporate. Drop by spoonful to greased cookie sheet. Press dough with back of fork dampened by water so it will not stick. Bake at 375° for 6-8 minutes. Will be thin and crisp. Store in tin or jar. Makes at least 3-4 dozen.

Marcia Wiltshire

Peach & Blueberry Crisp

5 cups peeled, sliced peaches
1 pint blueberries
2-4 tablespoons sugar (depends on desired sweetness)
1/2 cup rolled oats

1/2 cup brown sugar
1/4 cup flour
1/4 teaspoon cinnamon
1/4 cup butter, melted

Combine first 3 ingredients and put in greased 10"x10" pan. Mix the rest of the ingredients together and put on top of the peach-blueberry mixture. Bake 30 minutes at 375°. Serves 8.

Carolyn Sauve

Pears in Red Wine

1 cup dry red wine
1/2 cup sugar
1 cinnamon stick
1 bay leaf

1/2 teaspoon vanilla or vanilla bean
4 ripe Bosc pears

Combine wine, sugar, cinnamon stick, bay leaf and vanilla. Cut thin slice from bottom of each pear so it will stand upright. Place pears and wine mixture in round baking dish. Bake at 350°, basting frequently, 45-55 minutes. Remove bay leaf and vanilla bean, if used. Cool. Spoon sauce onto dessert plate. Add pear and vanilla ice cream, plus mint. Serves 4.

Jean Barclay

Pecan Pie

1 tablespoon butter
1 cup brown sugar
2 tablespoons flour
1 cup light corn syrup
3 eggs, beaten
1/4 teaspoon salt
1 teaspoon vanilla
1 cup pecan halves
1 unbaked pie shell

Cream butter with sugar and flour. Add syrup and eggs. Beat until frothy. Add salt, vanilla and pecan halves. Pour into 9-inch unbaked pie shell. Bake for 40 minutes at 325°. Serves 6-8.

Frances Landau

Perfect Apple Pie

2 MacIntosh apples
3-4 Granny Smith apples
3/4-1 cup sugar
2 tablespoons flour
1/8 teaspoon salt
1 teaspoon ground cinnamon
1/4 teaspoon freshly ground nutmeg
2 tablespoons butter
2 prepared pie crusts
Milk and extra sugar for glaze

Mix dry ingredients and sprinkle 1/2 over bottom crust in pie plate. Peel, core and slice apples. Heap into pastry shell and sprinkle with remaining dry mix. Dot with butter. Coat pastry edge with ice water. Cover pie with top crust. Pinch edges, fold under and flute to seal. Brush top crust with milk and sprinkle with sugar to glaze. Cut decorative steam vents in top. Bake 45 minutes in 400°. Serves 8.

Joyce Vitelli

Pound Cake

1 cup granulated sugar	1/4 teaspoon baking soda
1/4 pound butter	1/2 teaspoon baking powder
2 eggs	1/2 cup buttermilk
11/2 cups sifted flour	1/2 teaspoon vanilla

Cream together sugar and butter. Sift dry ingredients together. Add eggs to creamed mixture and beat well. Add dry ingredients alternately with buttermilk. Add vanilla and mix well. Pour batter into greased 9"x5" loaf pan or 3 small 53/4"x53/4" loaf pans. Bake large loaf for 1 hour at 350° and smaller ones for about 40 minutes. Serves 8.

Marjory Uhlenburg

Pumpkin Chiffon

1 envelope unflavored gelatin
1/4 cup cold water
3 eggs, separated
1 cup sugar
11/4 cup canned pumpkin
1/2 cup milk
3/4 teaspoon cinnamon

1/2 teaspoon ginger
1/4 teaspoon nutmeg
1/8 teaspoon salt
Whipped cream, toasted
    almonds, broken up ginger-
    snaps, for garnish

Dissolve gelatin in water. Slightly beat egg yolks. Add 1/2 cup sugar, pumpkin, milk and spices. Cook over low heat until slightly thickened (like heavy cream). Cool. Add gelatin and water mixture. Beat egg whites until soft peaks begin to form. Add remaining sugar. Continue to beat until stiff, but not dry. Stir 1 or 2 tablespoons of whites into pumpkin mixture, then fold in remaining whites. Divide mixture into individual martini glasses. Refrigerate until firm. Garnish before serving. Serves 8-10.

Phyllis Liebman

Raspberry Chocolate Cake

12 ounces chocolate chips

3/4 cup walnuts, chopped

1 package any chocolate cake
   mix with pudding

4 eggs

1/2 cup oil

1 teaspoon vanilla

1 package instant chocolate
   pudding mix

1 cup sour cream

1 pound bag frozen
   raspberries, defrosted

Optional Glaze:

2 squares unsweetened
   chocolate

1 square semi-sweet chocolate

2 tablespoons butter

2 tablespoons honey

1 teaspoon vanilla

If cake is wrapped in foil and plastic wrap, it will stay fresh for 2 days. Freezes well.

Defrost raspberries. Grease and flour tube or bundt pan. Preheat oven to 350°. Coat nuts and chips with 1 tablespoon cake mix. Set aside. Combine cake mix, eggs, oil, vanilla, pudding mix and sour cream in large bowl of automatic mixer and blend for 3 minutes on medium speed. Fold in coated chips and nuts. Fold in raspberries and their juices. Turn in prepared pan. Bake for 1 hour or until knife inserted in center of pan comes out clean. Cool for 30 minutes and turn out on cake rack or serving platter. Melt glaze ingredients together slowly. Drizzle while still warm over top and sides of cake. For special occasions, surround cake with fresh raspberries garnished with a few green holly or lemon leaves. Serves 10.

Sandra Roth

Rugelach

2 cups flour

1/2 pound Land O' Lakes light butter

1 (8 ounce) package cream cheese, 1/3 less fat

2 tablespoons cinnamon

1/2 cup raisins

6 tablespoons sugar

1/2 cup chopped walnuts

8 ounces raspberry preserves

Combine flour, butter and cream cheese. Wrap in wax paper and refrigerate for 24 hours. Cut the dough into 4 equal parts. Roll out one section at a time (flatten out like a small pizza). Mix cinnamon, raisins, sugar and walnuts. Spread preserves over dough. Add mixture of cinnamon, raisins, sugar and nuts. Sprinkle over dough. Cut dough into 16 equal sections. Roll to center. Place on a cookie sheet. Bake at 350° for 1/2 hour. Sprinkle with powdered sugar when done. Makes approximately 48 pieces.

Edythe Cohen

Rum Cake

1 cup chopped pecans
1 (181/2 ounce) package
   yellow cake mix
1 (31/2 ounce) package vanilla
   pudding
4 eggs
1/2 cup water
1/2 cup vegetable oil

1/2 cup dark rum

Glaze:
1/2 cup butter
1/4 cup water
1 cup granulated sugar
1/2 cup dark rum

This dessert improves with time!

Grease and flour 10-inch tube pan. Sprinkle nuts over bottom of pan. Mix all cake ingredients and pour batter over nuts. Bake at 325° for 1 hour. Cool. Invert onto serving plate. Melt butter. Stir in water and sugar. Boil over medium heat for 10 minutes, stirring constantly and slowly. Remove from heat. Stir in rum, then cool. To glaze cake, prick top with fork. Spoon and brush glaze. Allow cake to stand. Brush remaining glaze on top and sides. Serves 10-12.

Jean Barclay

Sand Tarts

1/2 pound butter
1/2 cup sifted confectioners
   sugar
2 cups cake flour

1 cup chopped pecans
1 teaspoon vanilla
Powdered sugar

Everyone south of New York makes these at Christmastime. They keep forever.

Preheat oven to 325°. Cream butter, then add sugar. Stir well; add flour, nuts and vanilla. Shape into balls or crescents and bake on ungreased cookie sheets for 20 minutes or until a light brown. Roll in powdered sugar while warm.

Dorothy Graebner

Seven Layer Cake

1 stick butter, melted
1 cup graham cracker crumbs
1 cup angel flake coconut
1 (6 ounce) chocolate bits
1 (6 ounce) butterscotch bits
1 can Borden condensed milk
1 cup chopped nuts

Spread each ingredient evenly and bake at 325° for 30 minutes in an 8"x8" square pan. Cool and cut bite-size, as it is very rich. Serves 8.

Joyce Kohl

Strawberries with Mascarpone Cheese

1/2 cup softened mascarpone cheese
3 tablespoons powdered sugar
1 tablespoon 1% low-fat milk
1 pint strawberries, hulled and sliced
1 cup coarsely crushed almond Biscotti amaretto cookies
Mint sprigs, optional

In a small bowl combine cheese, 1 tablespoon sugar and milk; mix well. In large bowl, combine strawberries and remaining 2 tablespoons powdered sugar. Spoon into 4 dessert goblets, stemmed. Spoon cheese mixture over strawberries; sprinkle with crushed biscotti. Serve immediately or cover and chill up to 2 hours before serving. Garnish with mint strips if desired. Serves 4.

Hella Mears Hueg

Swedish Nuts

5 cups pecan halves   1/4 teaspoon salt
1/2 cup butter   1 cup sugar
2 egg whites

Toast nuts in shallow pan in preheated 300° oven until lightly browned. Melt butter in a 15"x10"x1" pan in oven. Both pans can be in the oven at the same time. Beat egg whites and salt until soft peaks are formed. Gradually add sugar, while beating mixture. Fold hot toasted nuts into meringue. Spread evenly over melted butter in pan. Bake in preheated 300° oven for 30 minutes, stirring at 10-minute intervals. Cool and store in airtight container.

Ruth Thiel

Tiramisu Lite

2/3 cup powdered sugar

8 ounces low-fat cream cheese

1/2 cup sugar

1/4 cup water

3 egg whites

2 cups frozen low-fat cream, whipped and divided

1/2 cup hot water

1 tablespoon sugar

1 tablespoon strong coffee

2 tablespoons Kahlua or rum

2 dozen ladyfingers, split lengthwise

1 teaspoon unsweetened cocoa

1 ounce semi-sweet chocolate, shaved

Beat powdered sugar and cream cheese together in bowl. In double boiler, combine sugar, 1/4 cup water and egg whites. Over simmering water, beat with beater or whisk until custard is stiff. Gently stir in 1/4 of custard into cream cheese mixture. Then fold in remainder of custard. Fold in 1 cup whipped cream and set aside. Combine hot water, coffee, sugar and Kahlua or rum. In 3-inch dish, place half of ladyfingers, cut size up. Drizzle with half of Kahlua mixture. Spread 1/2 of cheese mixture over ladyfingers. Repeat layers of lady fingers, Kahlua mixture and cream cheese mixture. Spread remaining cup of cream whip. Dust with cocoa and shavings of chocolate. Refrigerate for 2 hours. Freeze 2 hours before serving. Serves 8-10.

Weezie Windsor

Toni's Walnut Cake

11 eggs, separated
11/2 cups sugar
11/2 teaspoons vanilla
3 cups walnuts, finely ground
12 zwiebacks, finely ground
11/2 teaspoons baking powder
3/4 teaspoon salt

Filling:
1/4 pound butter
1/4 pound confectioners sugar
1 egg
1 teaspoon vanilla
1/4 pound Nestle's milk
   chocolate, melted

To make the cake, beat egg yolks, sugar and vanilla until thick and creamy. Add ground walnuts, zwiebacks and baking powder. Add salt to egg whites and beat until stiff. Fold into the walnut mixture. Place in 2 well-buttered wax-lined 9-inch layer cake pans. Bake at 350° for about 30 minutes. For the filling, beat the last 4 ingredients until thick and creamy. Fold in melted chocolate. Can be frozen. Serves 12.

Eleanor Russo

Venetian Biscotti

My friend's mom who lives in Venice shared this recipe with me.

4 ounces semi-sweet chocolate, chopped in small pieces

1 cup sugar

11/2 cups flour

1/3 cup unsweetened cocoa

1 teaspoon baking soda

1/4 teaspoon salt

3 eggs

1 teaspoon vanilla

3/4 cup walnuts

Preheat oven to 300°. Sift together sugar, flour, cocoa, baking soda and salt. Combine eggs and vanilla. Add 1/2 of dry ingredients, then add walnuts. Add remaining dry ingredients including chocolate pieces. It will make stiff dough. Form 12-inch logs. (They will spread when baked.) Bake for 50 minutes. Let cool for 10 minutes. Cut into diagonal slices about 1/2 an inch thick or thicker. Bake 25 minutes more on one side, then flip and bake 12 minutes more on other side. Cool and enjoy. They should be crisp. Makes about 2 dozen.

Bobbie Lublin

Viennese Brownies

2 eggs

1 cup sugar

1/2 cup butter

2 squares unsweetened chocolate

1 teaspoon vanilla

1 cup flour, sifted

1/2 teaspoon baking powder

1/2 cup sliced almonds

Filling:

1 package cream cheese

1/3 cup sugar

1 egg

1/2 teaspoon almond extract

Beat eggs and sugar well. Melt butter with chocolate; cool slightly. Add chocolate butter to egg mixture. Add vanilla. Gradually stir in flour sifted with baking powder. For the filling, soften cream cheese and beat sugar, egg and flavoring. Spread half of brownie mixture on bottom of greased 9"x9" baking pan. Spread filling over it. Spread remaining brownie batter over filling. Sprinkle top with almond slices. Bake in preheated 350° oven for 30 minutes. Serves 8.

Barbara Bloomstrom

Vinegar Pie

2 tablespoons butter

1/2 cup sugar

3 tablespoons flour

1 teaspoon cinammon

1/4 teaspoon powdered cloves

1/4 teaspoon allspice

1/8 teaspoon salt

1 egg

2 tablespoons vinegar

1 cup water

Joe Hirshhorn's favorite.

Mix all ingredients in top of double boiler. Cook over boiling water, stirring constantly (about 8 minutes). Cool. Pour into small baked pie shell. Bake at 350° for 12 minutes. Serves 6-8.

Olga Hirshhorn

APPLAUSE

WE RECEIVED AN OVERWHELMING RESPONSE OF ALMOST 800 recipes! However, we regret that due to lack of space and similarity, we were unable to include each and every one. If your recipe does not appear, please consider it still your secret, but know that we will keep it on file when planning our next cookbook.

More than 400 recipes, representing 13 categories, were published. Featured are the "tried and true" and the "must try" recipes from the Friends of the Philharmonic including the volunteers from both the Naples Philharmonic League and Friends of Art, Philharmonic supporters, board members, staff, musicians and artists. We are grateful for your submissions and hope that your favorites will be included in upcoming meals and dinner parties by the collectors of this cookbook.

On behalf of the Cookbook Steering Committee, we would like to applaud those who dedicated their time and talent to the success of this project. Their names are listed below. Everyone from the visionary (Myra Janco Daniels) to the judges, testers, staff, underwriter and contract publisher deserves a standing ovation.

Cookbook Steering Committee

Jean Barclay
Leslie Branda
Joann Duncan
Lynne Groth

Grace Seitz
Lori Sherman
Ruth Thiel
Kay Wing

Acknowledgements

CEO & Cookbook Visionary
Myra Janco Daniels

Judges & Testers

Jean Barclay
Leslie Branda

Lin Chandler
Noreen Cleasen

Adrienne Cozette
Joann Duncan
Mary Alice French
Char Macaluso
Mary McComas
Nancy Porter
Jan Ross

Grace Seitz
Klea Shiff
Helen Stephens
Ruth Thiel
Babs Tucker
Kay Wing

Philharmonic Center Staff

Ashley Carter
Laura Clemo
John Garbo
Jim Lilliefors

Darlene McCloud
Naomi Morris
Pat Plescia
Pablo Veintimilla

Volunteers

Jay Barclay
Carol Conant
Lea Mendel
Gail Webster-Patterson

Virginia Small
Joyce Stack
Virginia Quirk

Gulfshore Life

Meg Caetano
Jessica Grace
Lynne Groth
Kay Kipling
Kellie Lavin

Kathleen Peckham
Tracy Heaslip Ross
Jocelyn Stevens
Tricia Tarantino
Jamie Withrow

Special Thanks

Don Eddy,
Cover Artist
Judy and Noah Liff,
Photorealism Exhibit Donors
Glen Harrell,
Waterside Shops at Pelican Bay

Joanne Walsh & Kelly Jacoby,
Saks Fifth Avenue
Michael Goodman,
Bitner.com

Index

ORDER FORMS

MAIL TO:

Philharmonic Center for the Arts, Attn: *The Art of Cooking*, 5833 Pelican Bay Blvd., Naples, FL 34108.

Make checks payable to: Philharmonic Center for the Arts

Please send _____ copies of *The Art of Cooking* @ $19.95 each ....$ _____

6% sales tax for Florida residents or $1.20 each...$ _____

Postage & handling $5.50 (first copy) $1.00 (each additional copy).......................$ _____

TOTAL ENCLOSED $ _____

Name _____

Address _____

City _____ State _____ ZIP _____

Daytime Phone _____

☐ Payment Enclosed　　☐ VISA　　☐ MC　　☐ AMEX　　☐ DISCOVER

Credit Card # _____ Exp. Date _____

Signature _____

Please allow 2 weeks for delivery.

Proceeds from the sale of this book will be used to support the Naples Philharmonic League and Friends of Art, to benefit the Orchestra and Museum Endowment Funds.

- -

MAIL TO:

Philharmonic Center for the Arts, Attn: *The Art of Cooking*, 5833 Pelican Bay Blvd., Naples, FL 34108.

Make checks payable to: Philharmonic Center for the Arts

Please send _____ copies of *The Art of Cooking* @ $19.95 each ....$ _____

6% sales tax for Florida residents or $1.20 each...$ _____

Postage & handling $5.50 (first copy) $1.00 (each additional copy).......................$ _____

TOTAL ENCLOSED $ _____

Name _____

Address _____

City _____ State _____ ZIP _____

Daytime Phone _____

☐ Payment Enclosed　　☐ VISA　　☐ MC　　☐ AMEX　　☐ DISCOVER

Credit Card # _____ Exp. Date _____

Signature _____

Please allow 2 weeks for delivery.

Proceeds from the sale of this book will be used to support the Naples Philharmonic League and Friends of Art, to benefit the Orchestra and Museum Endowment Funds.